Performing Literary Texts

The Challenge of Chamber Theatre.

Roy B. Tabor

Tanfield House

ISBN: 978-1-291-37439-1

Published in London, 2013

"What revels are in hand. Is there no play
To ease the anguish of a torturing hour?

Say, what abridgement have you for this evening?
What masque, what music? How shall we beguile
The lazy time if not with some delight?"

Shakespeare, A Midsummer Night's Dream, V, sc.1, 36

"Work, work your thoughts,
Be kind
And eke out our performance with your mind".

Shakespeare, Henry V. 3.1 Prologue.

"Oh, do not ask, 'What is it?'
Let us go and make our visit".

T.S.Eliot, The Love Song of J. Alfred Prufrock.

The Author

Roy Tabor, MBE, has long experience in theatre both as actor and director. An early acquaintance with studio theatre led to arranging and directing a production of '*John Brown's Body*' in chamber theatre style. This was followed later by similar arrangements of Chaucer's *Canterbury Tales*; ten of the *Tales* have been presented in the authentic medieval manner as 'The Chaucer Experience'. Since then he has created numerous other scripts for performance in this style. His work has taken him to South Africa, The Philippines, Sri Lanka, Canada, U.S.A. and the West Indies. He is the author of the *T-Script* shorthand method.

for

Margaret

A lifetime of love and caring.

CONTENTS

Introduction

Performing literature is a way of exploring human life and behaviour in the form of entertainment. This book is intended for everyone who is interested in literature – poetry, prose or drama – and who wishes to share that interest with others. It may be of particular interest to teachers and students, and to librarians, parents and theatre folk.

The concept of 'Literature in Performance' is explored and is set in its historical perspective. Some of the terms applied to this form of theatre are described and then the techniques of reading aloud as a performance are introduced.

What emerges is a world of exploration of the human mind and behaviour and that greatest attribute of mankind – imagination. Indeed, for many, the preferred term for this exploration is '*Theatre of the Imagination*' where a literary work is performed without scenery, lighting or costumes. Through imagination the audience is caught up and intimately involved in the performance in a very special way.

Much has been written about 'literature in performance', the performance of a literary text with an audience. One form of presentation, Readers Theatre, is popular in schools in North America, where the primary focus is on classroom activities; the aim there is to stimulate young persons' interests in books and reading.

Less has been written on the adult focus in performing literature although the technique of performing texts may be used in university language and literature departments. This form of theatre has been given several names and each one tends to focus upon a particular aspect of presentation; the term used in this book is 'Chamber Theatre'. This is an intimate performance style where a handful of players perform with audiences in small venues, including in a Host's drawing-room.

The performer of chamber theatre is an 'actor/storyteller' who shares a story with an audience as intimates and includes narration in a 'conversational' performance mode. In contrast, the stage actor in a play performs at a distance in front of a larger audience using the dialogue of the characters in the story; the professional actor is required to undergo rigorous training in breath control, speech and movement to enable performing on a variety of public stages.

This book is not concerned with examinations, medals or diplomas in reading, speaking or acting. That is a different purpose. Here, the intention is to explore literature for enjoyment and entertainment through performance, sharing the pleasure with others. In these pages you will find suggestions of how a literary text may be performed with an audience present. The performer 'breathes life and meaning into the words for the pleasure of the audience'.

This is the world of chamber theatre, an ancient form of theatre with a contemporary face. It is theatre centred on the imagination without the costs of conventional stage productions; it is a demanding form of theatre but with great opportunities for both players and their audiences.

Performing Literary Texts
The Challenge of Chamber Theatre.

Part One: Concept and Perspective.

1. Story-telling.

Words, words, words . . . the tools of human communication. Our spoken and written language is made up of words – thousands of them. Using words we communicate our thoughts, feelings and intentions to others.

Yet words are only one tool of communication. Like all animals we have ways of non-verbal communication; these may be simple indicators of gesture or sound (a warning growl or a mew for help) or more sophisticated messages such as the 'dancing instruction' of honey bees indicating where to find flowers in bloom.

Consider the sentence,

> *" . . . and then she looked at me and my heart stopped . . .".*

The words convey to the reader the specific action of looking, but the words also indicate a subtext which we interpret through our own imagination. That interpretation of how '*she looked*' and the effect on '*my heart*' is based on our own personal knowledge and experience. Words are used to express our feelings and emotions.

Then, beyond the written words there is a further dimension of interpretation. We may suppose a pause in the narrative before the beginning of the sentence and another pause at the end. These are dramatic pauses indicated by the punctuation that convey added meaning to the words; another pause might be inserted between '*me*' and '*and*' to increase tension and effect. Try saying this sentence aloud in different ways to indicate different meanings – be aware of any intuitive gestures or facial expressions that you find yourself making (the pronoun '*she*' may be inter-changed with '*he*').

In the following chapters we will explore the complex world of words as tools of communication and we will consider how the impact of words may be modified through the use of non-verbal actions. This exploration is set in the context of 'Literature in Performance' – the communication of ideas and experiences through the medium of written words transformed into speech.

The term 'Literature' is interpreted widely to include all types of written material, e.g. books, magazine articles, reports and ephemera, and also all forms of presentation (prose, poetry and drama). The term 'Performing literature' is used to mean the interpretation of a written text through speech and action before an audience; the act of performance is an essential element of interpretation of the text.

An original text is the product of an author (or a collaboration of authors) and derives from personal experience, knowledge or belief. These are the influences on the author's choice of words and the manner in which they are composed. We can begin the interpretation of a written text with an understanding of the author – the background and the perceived intentions for writing the work, this is the 'author context'. When we begin to read the text itself we enter the 'reader context'; this is where our own life experience and imagination become involved in the interpretation.

Reading a text *silently* will give a first-level understanding of what the author has written but some words and even whole passages may not be given due value. Reading *aloud* brings each word into focus with greater awareness of meaning. However, it is only when a text is read aloud *to an audience* that deeper understanding occurs. The audience may consist of only a single person but this reading aloud becomes an act of performance requiring interpretation of the text.

Many words have been written about the relationships of the text and the performance (the reader-response), and about the nature of the 'audience' (the audience response). Much of that discussion has focussed on stage plays as the vehicle of 'performance' but there has been less written about 'reading-aloud' literary texts as performance. The audience at a performance of a literary text is similar to a theatre audience, both 'performances' are forms of story-telling but whereas the play-script is presented as dialogue, the literary text will include narration combined with dialogue.

For present purposes 'literature in performance' is regarded as 'acted oral story-telling'. This is a performance usually intended for entertainment but it has an added value when used in education. Gillian Clarke, the Welsh poet, considers story-telling as performing, like dancing or acting, but some contemporary story-tellers have been resistant to the notion that story-telling is a form of acting. Jill Balcon, actress and teacher of speech, considered poetry reading as a distinct art from acting (1). Her reasoning is that no performing art can be learnt from a book; unlike music which has performance notation, reading poetry has no marks to guide how it is to be read. Instead, the phrasing and lyric impulse are a submission of the reader's self and these have to be drawn out of someone in whom they do exist. When a literary text (poetry or prose) is read aloud to an audience the reader applies his or her own life experience to the presentation and this interpretation of the words can be described as a performance.

Oral story-telling.

When we tell a story to another person that is an act of performance. It is oral story-telling and falls within the comprehensive and general term of 'literature in performance'; this general term has numerous facets that have each acquired various descriptions and some of these are described in the following chapters. Performing literature has been widely discussed as 'oral interpretation' and, as Sonkowsky pointed out, it has been described as the queen over all tributary literary studies such as philology (2). Homer has for long been understood to be the father of oral interpretation in the western world but there were many poet-performers before Homer. Both the *Iliad* and the *Odyssey* derive from pre-literate oral tradition. Before such early poems were written down they were recited aloud; probably they were never 'fixed' but received a different version at each performance. Those early metrical compositions were sung and many were associated with particular musical instruments such as the lyre; as dramatic works came into vogue with spoken episodes interspersed between song, often choral, acting gradually became as important as singing.(3).

There is a long history of oral story-telling with origins deep in man's past. Once humans had become erect and had acquired the ability to speak, their early communication may have started with sounds specific to an occasion, such as warning, fear or command. Such elemental sounds became organised as words and associated with particular actions and activities such as hunting and food gathering and then, in due course, words to express emotions and feelings gradually developed.

From existing primitive societies we can extrapolate something of the early development of language in which word sounds were combined with gestures and body movements. Early language is likely to have been related to the essential aspects of existence, hunting and gathering of food. During periods of rest and relaxation there would be opportunities to bond the community together with questions and answers about the general issues of daily life and of the physical world. Inevitably this would have included talk about the mysterious events of day and night, sun, moon and stars, fire and storm; with only limited knowledge, inevitably speculation followed and folklore began to emerge.

It is here that one can see the emergence of man and the distinction from other animals. It is the use of the imagination that sets man apart from other animals. This vital difference has provided the wealth of myths and folklore which over centuries has permeated all societies of mankind and which continues to develop and influence our actions.

Early story-telling influenced cultural and social beliefs and the whole gamut of human inter-action which, in turn, influenced later story-telling. In this way the group's history and culture was passed on to new generations. Factual knowledge was very limited and the stories would have been derived from local and personal experiences and modified by imagination. An increase in factual knowledge may have had less influence on story development as we find that throughout these myths there is a continuing thread of magic and fantasy; even with the extent of knowledge in the twenty-first century and the discounting of magical events there is continuing interest in fantasy and myth.

Before the invention of writing these stories formed man's oral culture, the stories were told, memorized and re-told. The core elements remained constant but modifications were introduced. This process can be described as *creative story-telling*; in each re-telling words and gestures were used appropriate to each audience. Modern story-tellers continue the ancient practice and are highly skilled in entertaining and in stimulating the imaginations of their audiences. A story may be taken from a written source or from hearing it from another story-teller. It is then reworked according to the story-teller's skills and presented to a new audience using words appropriate to the listeners.

Written story-telling.
In our contemporary society the printed book is ubiquitous in cheap and accessible forms. Currently newer forms are becoming available in electronic (digital) forms. These written texts are intended primarily for silent reading. This places emphasis on the level of literacy, knowledge and experience of the individual reader and is thus related to levels and quality of education. The silent reader is a single and personal interpreter of the story.

Technology has enabled a written text to be performed for a 'silent' reader by means of the audio-book. In this format the reader of the original text records his own personal interpretation which may not relate to the listener's experience. A recording by the author of the work may be regarded as an authoritative interpretation of the text. However, such recordings are time and place specific; subsequent recordings may show some evolution of thought and the presentations may use different inflections or emphasis which can be informative. Not all authors are fluent readers.

Every written story text requires interpretation. The silent reader makes his own interpretation following the indications provided by the author in the vocabulary used and the punctuation employed. However, all written texts achieve added value to their interpretation when they are read aloud and this has led to a number of contemporary approaches to the process of crafted story-telling.

The art of creative story-telling is distinguished from 'literature in performance' (the performance of a written work). The skill of the creative story-teller is to take a memorized story and engage an audience in a new telling. 'Performing literature' takes a story (this may be in the form of prose, poetry or drama) which has been carefully crafted by its original author, and then to present the author's own words to a new audience with an imaginative and interpretative performance; this is *crafted story-telling*. The intention is that the presenter of the crafted text will visualize and interpret the words in a similar way to the perceived images in the author's mind. This performance is based on an understanding and appreciation of the author's choice of vocabulary, writing style and punctuation. The crafted story enables listeners to hear the story more closely to the way in which it was written and presumably intended to be heard. The audience-response will then have an additional influence on the presentation.

Performance mode.
The significance of this telling of the crafted story in 'performance mode' can be understood by comparing it with normal silent reading of a text. When reading silently, often some passages of text may be glossed over, for example, long passages of description. In dialogue sections the reporting clauses may also be 'skipped' ('*he said*', '*she replied*') and the full force of the manner of speaking is thus modified.

If the same text is now read *aloud*, a new dimension is apparent. The reader is forced to read and speak every word that has been written; this slows down the reading process but each word is given its own value. The result is nearer to the 'crafted intentions' of the author as there is now time to absorb and interpret the words. The reporting clauses can now be interpreted by inflection as they occur – in the sentence "*I can't do it, she sobbed*", the words "*she sobbed*" would then be spoken with the appropriate emotion.

A further dimension emerges if the text is now read aloud ***to an audience***; the reading becomes a performance. The audience may consist of a single person or a number of listeners. In performance mode the reader introduces his or her own personal interpretation of the author's words. Such interpretation will be influenced by the reader's own knowledge and experience. This act of performance will be preceded by some preparation by the reader-performer who will read through the text and note the manner in which the story is presented. As a result of this preparation the dialogue words "*I can't do it*" can be interpreted and spoken in the manner of sobbing and the reporting clause, "*she sobbed*" is read as narration without inflection.

We can conclude that performing a text enables interpretation of the words to follow more closely the author's intentions in creating characterisation and to realise the action. Because the audience becomes involved when participating in a performance the story becomes memorable and has greater impact than when it is read silently. Silent reading is the norm today in our literate society but it is a sad reflection that many people, though literate, are not fluent readers and do not read for pleasure. This is not a new phenomenon; similar experience has been seen in earlier generations and was a feature of the 'Penny Readings' movement of the late nineteenth century.

Reading aloud, though rarely practised when reading a book, is more likely when reading poetry. You cannot fully appreciate the physical and sensual nature of the words of a poem until you speak them aloud. Cicely Berry is outspoken on this point; "speaking poetry is valuable to the actor . . . as it increases the sensibility to words, and rhythms and meanings which come to you from sound" (4). The poet Basil Bunting is equally explicit, "Poetry lies dead on the page, until some voice brings it to life (5)

Literature in performance.
Performing literature is essentially the exploration and interpretation of a literary text in performance mode – in simple terms, 'reading aloud to an audience'.

An overview of the elements of 'Literature in Performance' is presented in fig.1.

Literature in Performance

The exploration / interpretation of a literary text in performance mode.
(Reading aloud to an audience.)

AUTHOR	**PRESENTER**	**AUDIENCE**
(Originator)	(Interpreter)	(Listening with Imagination)

Literary Forms

Poetry	Prose	Drama

Presentation Forms

Oral	Written	Movement
(spoken / sung)	(recorded)	(dance / mime)

Fig. 1.

The Author is the originator of the text (story), the Presenter interprets the story using a range of communication skills, and the Audience, the essential third element in performance, listens to the story using their own personal contributions of imagination and experience. The literary text may be presented through speech (direct reading of the story), by recording the story (this becomes a new format beyond the original written text), or the story may be told through movement (dance or mime).

The elements of *Interpretation* are seen in Fig 2. (next page)

'Literature in Performance'

Interpretation

STORY-TELLER	NARRATOR / READER	ACTOR
The 'creative story'	The 'crafted story'	Dialogue with action
(Adapts a memorized story and recreates it for a particular audience)	(Original words are used)	(Original words but joint interpretation)

Presentation method

Silent reading	Reading aloud	Play (stage)
Reader's personal interpretation	Narrator's interpretation	Joint interpretation - Author's Dialogue & Stage directions Director & Actor Scenery / staging, Lighting, Costumes, Accessories, Make-up / Masks

Fig. 2.

The creative story-teller adapts a memorized story and presents it to a particular audience using words that are appropriate to the audience, but when a story crafted by the original author is read aloud to an audience, the carefully written text is interpreted through the reading skills of the presenter. A performed story-text is not a play. In a dramatic text (a play script) each actor interprets a specific character in the play using the given dialogue but influenced by personal insight (through study and experience) into the character's thoughts and actions. This is further interpreted through the stage setting, costumes and make-up.

Most often a crafted story is written for the 'author's audience' with the probability of silent reading; the reader finds clues to the author's meaning given in the language used and in the narrative, and applies his own personal interpretation of the written words. When a crafted story is performed to an audience the text is interpreted by the Narrator/Performer through voice and gesture to communicate character, location and action; this brings the story more vividly into focus. As Professor Evelyn Vitz puts it, the act of performing "breathes life into the text" (6).

The play-script.
In a stage play the story is presented through dialogue; the characters in the play tell the story by speaking to each other. Each actor is assigned a specific character/role and endeavours to interpret the words of the

dialogue text in the manner of the assumed character. This brings the text to life as a 'real-time' event of entertainment.

The significance of performance was understood by Sir Richard Baker (1634) who declared that "a play read hath not half the pleasure of a Play acted; for though it have the pleasure of ingenious speeches, yet it wants the pleasure of Graceful action . . . Graceful action is the greatest pleasure of a play".

Gross (7) has pointed out that the play-script is a hypothetical play, a springboard for interpretation, not to be confused with the play that will eventually be staged; the 'meaning' and 'hypothetical play' are 'mental events evoked by words, not the words themselves. Berry writes that poetry, "purely by the associations of words and rhythms can penetrate the sub-conscious understanding. Language itself reacts on us" (8). This view is endorsed by Martin Esslin, "a dramatic text, unperformed, is literature, it can be read as a story", the distinguishing element is that of *'performance'* or enactment (9). The audience becomes the critical factor in the process of performance.

The story-line of an acted play is presented by dialogue and developed through the theatrical narration of the stage setting, scenery and lighting, and through the costumes and make-up of the actors. This involves a range of interpreters and interpretive devices including the author's stage directions. The Director's personal oversight will be supported and extended by each actor's own insight, experience and skill; together, these form the 'basic narration' of the play. The author (playwright) may provide specific 'narration' by describing the physical setting or the personalities and movements of the characters. The costumes, accessories, make-up or masks provide 'character narration'. Both Ibsen and Bernard Shaw wrote extended narrative background into their play-scripts.

There are other forms of a story-play but all include the basic elements of narration and dialogue; a ballet is a story presented through music and dance movement. Here, the narration and dialogue are provided through the movements and the interactions of the dancers but the attendant features of scenery, lighting and costume are similar in purpose and effect to the acted stage play. Other performed stories include opera, musicals and mime; in these forms of story-telling the 'dialogue' does not require spoken words but may be provided through singing or silent movement.

Reading aloud.

Although many parents read stories aloud to their children, as these young persons learn to read for themselves they gravitate to silent reading. With only limited experience of life the young reader has to use imagination to begin to make sense of the story. If the story is read aloud, greater understanding of the text can follow. The act of reading aloud requires an active personal interpretation by the reader and stimulates imagination and feelings. For this reason young persons should be encouraged to read at least some portions of the story aloud.

Reading aloud, as performed literature, requires an audience, a minimum of one, but, as this tends to be an intimate event, the numbers of the audience will have an influence on its interpretation. This limitation is explored later (Chamber Theatre) together with some comments on the advantages of the intimate occasion as a shared experience.

A distinction can thus be made between 'performing literature' (or 'literature in performance') and the conventional stage play. But the fundamental elements of story-telling have remained constant throughout history; there is always a creator of the story, an adapter/presenter and an audience – a group of individuals who listen with their imaginations and their personal experiences.

Various names have been used to describe these forms of 'literature in performance' (texts read aloud to an audience); each different name used is an attempt to focus on a particular aspect of presentation, e.g. Readers Theatre, Interpreter's Theatre, Platform Theatre, Concert Reading, Staged Reading and Drama of the Living Voice. The essential and common elements of all these are – reading the text aloud, performing before an audience, and stimulating the imaginations of the audience to visualize the setting of the story. Some of these contemporary forms of performance and their particular features are detailed later. But first the crafted story is viewed in a brief historical perspective.

Notes.
1. Jill Balcon, quoted by Josephine A. Johnson *Return of the Scops*, in Thompson, David W. *Performance of Literature in historical perspective*, (Lanham, MD, University Press of America, 1983), p.309.
2. Robert F. Sonkowsky, *Oral Performance in Ancient Greek Literature*, in Thompson, David W. ibid, p1.
3. Robert F. Sonkowsky, ibid, p.12.
4. Cicely Berry, *Voice and the actor*, (New York, NY, Wiley, 1973), p101.
5. Basil Bunting, quoted by Josephine Johnson *Return of the Scops*, in Thompson, ibid, p.304.

6. Evelyn Bauer Vitz, *Teaching Arthur through performance*, (Arthuriana 15, 2005).
7. Gross, Roger, *Understanding play-scripts; theory and method*, (Bowling Green, OH, Bowling Green University, 1974), p.41.
8. Berry, ibid, p.102.
9. Martin Esslin, *The Field of Drama*, (London, Methuen, 1987), p.24.

2. Historical perspectives – the crafted story.

Beginnings, cultural/oral literature
Before the introduction of writing, creative oral story-telling was the norm of popular entertainment; this practice continues to be seen today through the performances of many skilled story-tellers. For centuries stories and poetry were sung and often accompanied by musical instruments. Singing and rhyming were easy to remember but each performance would be different although in some societies the Shaman, as a cultural custodian in a particular social group, had a responsibility to memorize and recite long histories of the community.

Greek culture
Some three thousand years ago Greek culture lay at the heart of western civilization. For several centuries Greek thought laid the foundations for what was to become a Western European way of life and which was later to have global implications. The sung poems of early Greece were a continuation and development of earlier oral story-telling and entertainment. Although during this period many poems were committed to writing, each performance would not have been 'fixed' but would have been varied on each occasion. Spoken episodes were inserted between the sung sections, often performed as choral singing, until eventually speaking and acting became as important as singing. The original Greek 'actor' may have been the 'answerer' to the Chorus as the word may have meant 'interpreter' or 'explorer' (1). The Chorus sang or chanted the story and the 'actor' interpreted and developed the meaning in the words.

As Greece declined, the Roman Empire and its civilization became dominant and its power and influence was spread throughout the Western world by military conquest and settlement; this influence was to last many centuries. Latin, the language of the Romans, was spoken throughout the Empire and became the primary language of the Christian religion and of politics; the various vernaculars were the speech of the common people of each region or country.

In England, Anglo-Saxon was widely spoken at the time of the Roman incursion, but with much variation across the regions. The general population was illiterate but King Alfred (849-899) made great efforts to encourage literacy. He translated Bede's *Ecclesiastical History* into Anglo-Saxon and made a collection of the ancient heroic songs and poems of the North which were the common legacy of the Dane and Englishman

(2). Alfred has been called the father of English prose; he compiled handbooks on theology, history and geography. Alfred also founded the first 'public schools' for teaching letters to the sons of noblemen and thegns preparing them for the responsibility of administration. In the monasteries Alfred provided books to be read aloud and also provided a jewelled 'pointer' for the reader as an aid to keeping his eyes on the line he was reading.

But secular life was essentially an oral culture which underpinned the production and use of the written word. Popular entertainment included the singing and reciting by the 'scop', the Old English poet-performer. Their performances were highly theatrical and arresting and were presented in halls and villages usually to a noisy audience. The word 'scop' described the spontaneous making of a praise-worthy song.

Aldhelm, the seventh-century Abbot of Malmesbury is credited with the interweaving of the Christian scriptures with popular song. This link between the vernacular performance and Christian materials was fused by the poetry and song of Caedmon and was used to spread the teaching of the Church amongst the common people. The story is told of Caedmon's dream that a heavenly speaker appeared to him and commanded him to sing the scriptures. Although frowned upon by many in the Church hierarchy, the interaction of the illiterate oral performance of Caedmon and the literacy of the monastic world was to be significant in the way the Church spread its teaching and influence.

The Middle Ages and the written word.
The Middle English period is generally considered have begun from 1066 with the Norman invasion of England by William the Conqueror. The Middle Ages were a period of transition when the modern vernacular languages were fast emerging from speech into writing and were challenging the dominance of Latin. The 'High' language of Latin was used in religion, government and high culture generally, while the 'Low' vernacular language was used by the common people in their daily life; this duality of language (diglossia) was common throughout Western Europe. The impact of writing allowed stories to be passed on without reliance only on the oral story-tellers; this was a slow and gradual evolution and was linked both to the development of literacy in society and also to the evolving forms of written record – the clay tablet and papyrus roll had given way to the multi-leaved codex on parchment and paper.

The language of the (Roman) Church was Latin and the development of oral performance during the Middle Ages can be seen in the history of the Church. The Mass was celebrated in Latin by a priest who was distantly separated from the congregation. Without being able to understand the words, the people created their own meanings for the priest's actions and gestures and the celebrant became a performer for a distant audience. In the monasteries oral interpretation was encouraged by the reading aloud of sacred texts, especially during meal-times. The Benedictine Rule was read aloud to their novices in this way.

Oral performance was an important part of secular life as well as the monastic. Preaching the Christian message, particularly by the itinerant monks and friars, can be seen as being less of a religious activity and more as 'story-telling' within the oral narrative tradition (3) where the preacher is both teacher and entertainer and the bringer of news. Preaching manuals of the time directed the speaker to "speak slowly, distinctly and gravely. Do not look about aimlessly. Do not stand like a statue [nor] exaggerate your gestures" (4)

In church the preacher stood on the chancel steps; later, pulpits were built for this purpose for better viewing and hearing. In England the sermons were given in the vernacular. It was the mendicant friars who revolutionized the history of preaching; the Franciscans were dubbed "God's minstrels" recognising that they needed to use similar techniques to the then popular entertainers (minstrels). Gaining and keeping the audience's attention was always a difficult task in church and more so for preachers in the village square.

The term 'minstrels', applied to the general entertainers, also included the troubadours and the jonglars (in France, the 'jongleurs'). The 'troubadour' was a 'maker of music', often of high birth and literate; who composed sung 'epics' or tales of love and adventure. They either performed these 'epics' themselves to the accompaniment of a musical instrument or they were diffused more widely by the jonglars, the professional entertainers who were predominantly illiterate and were often regarded as disreputable characters.

The popular oral entertainment of the period was the telling and singing of the Romances, narratives of adventure. The Franciscans imitated the techniques of the minstrels and re-told the stories of man's salvation in simple understandable terms as entertainment. Verse and even popular songs were used as their preaching texts. This approach has been vividly encapsulated in Chaucer's Pardoner as he begins his story in *The Canterbury Tales*.

> *"In churches where I preach*
> *I cultivate a haughty kind of speech*
> *And ring it out as soundly as a bell;*
> *I've got it all by heart, the tale I tell.*
> *I have a text, it always is the same*
> *And always has been, since I learned the game.*
> Radix malorum est cupiditas".
> (trans. Neville Coghill, Penguin Books)

The late Middle Ages were times of momentous changes in English society. The signing of *Magna Carta* (1215) signalled the eventual demise of feudalism as a way of social organisation. The Great Plague of 1346-8 led to far-reaching upheavals in rural society; the Three Estates (Knight, Church and Serf), for long the foundation of English society, began a slow evolution of change. Language itself was changing; Norman-French (Anglo-French), spoken by the aristocracy and in government, began to be replaced by Middle English which was the general language of the people and there were several regional dialects. Latin still held domain in the affairs of the Church; this embraced theology, philosophy, science, medicine, law and government. Other, secular concerns remained to be expressed in the vernacular and, as society was changing rapidly, the language of the people grew in importance.

The written word evolved from speech, from the expression of thought and experience of everyday life to the infinite creativity of literature. The thirteenth and fourteenth centuries saw a gradual change from wide-spread oralcy to literacy, with the decline of song and the spoken 'epic' and the rising popularity of the 'Romance' stories of love and adventure. The Middle Ages are thus seen as an important period of transition when modern vernacular languages first emerged from speech into writing and began to challenge the dominance of Latin. There was an increasing literacy rate and the use of the written word in a still predominantly oral society. Early written stories in English had appeared in the fourteenth century, notably, Langland's *Piers Plowman*, and the anonymous *Sir Gawain and the Green Knight,* but it was the poet story-teller Geoffrey Chaucer who impacted the development of the English language and literature.

Like a meteor across the heavens Chaucer appeared in mid-century; he was born in 1343. A civil servant and a poet of distinction, Chaucer was a supreme story-teller writing in the language of the common people (he spoke and wrote in the London dialect of Middle English). His stories, collected as *The Canterbury Tales,* portrayed medieval life in a series of vivid and unforgettable characters; this was a water-shed in English literature. His use of the vernacular in his story-telling was a new and an arresting way to treat social issues.

After Chaucer's death in 1400, written communication took a major step forward with the introduction of printing to England in the second half of the fifteenth century. This led to important developments in story-telling with wider access to books, the evolution of the commercial theatre and the flowering of the English language. Subsequent developments have separated the basic elements of story-telling into written texts for reading (prose and poetry) and dramatised stories written to be performed as theatre. The introduction of the printing press enabled stories to be read with lessening reliance on oral transmission which had dominated story-telling for centuries. The significance of Chaucer on modern Chamber Theatre is explored in the next chapter.

Printing and the Renaissance.
Following the introduction of printing, oral story-telling began to lose its primary position in popular entertainment and edification; the reading of books and other printed material became a main source of information and the theatre became a special and different place of story-telling entertainment.

Nevertheless oralcy was never completely obscured by print. During the Renaissance good speaking and delivery became an important part of social role-playing. 'Courtesy' books taught the importance of good delivery and pronunciation (5). Attention was paid to the quality of the voice and advice given that it should be varied like a musical instrument; gesture was regarded as a factor in good delivery. Castiglione (6) considered the "ability to enact a story so important that it may be defined as civility itself", and Guazzo sees oral performance "as an ability that involves many of the skills of the orator or actor without participating of the exaggeration of either one". The lack of exaggeration is stressed because he is considering oral performance within the context of 'civil' or social conversation (7). During the Middle Ages oral interpretation had been mainly a skill of the professional minstrel, but now in the Renaissance it became a skill of the cultured person (8). This recognition is seen again in the latter part of the nineteenth century in England with the 'Penny Readings' movement (see below).

Story-telling in drama.

Story-telling through theatrical performances has undergone many changes during the past thousand years. Since the seventeenth century the English stage has been seen as a place, a platform, on which to perform a story, the form universally known as a 'play'. The Elizabethan stage saw both the burgeoning of the English language and the establishment of modern drama.

The early medieval Church had presented plays in church for biblical and doctrinal teaching. Then lay people became involved, but when the plays became too bawdy for the Church to allow inside the building and in front of the altar, the amateur players were pushed outside the building; firstly the players were relegated to performing outside on the church steps but later they were pushed further away. These performances moved into the village square where moveable platforms or pageants were used to stage often very elaborate spectacles sponsored by the various craft guilds. At the end of the fourteenth century, one of the early Morality plays, *The Lord's Prayer* (York cycle) so impressed the spectators that a company was formed to provide frequent performances of this play; this company comprised a hundred members and their wives (9)

By the sixteenth century the peripatetic stages of the village green had moved into one end of an inn yard which, in turn, led to permanent buildings – the Theatre. Tudor playwrights wrote plays for performance in the Rose, the Swan and the Globe theatres; this was the time of the flowering of the English language and the age of Marlowe, Johnson and Shakespeare. The open air thrust stages were subsequently roofed over and then later, with the introduction of artificial lighting, new techniques could be explored. This was accompanied by the development of the proscenium arch with the 'picture-frame' stage and a new style of theatre emerged. Here we see the marked demarcation between the actors who tell the story and the audience who may now be regarded as spectators looking in at the action.

The theatre continued to evolve during the seventeenth century in spite of the attempts of the Puritans to suppress it. Their eventual success to close the theatres was never complete and only temporary between 1642-1660 when eventually the monarchy was restored and the theatres re-opened.

During the eighteenth century there was much innovation in the presentation of plays. Elaborate scenery was introduced and mechanical devices were used to enhance the stage settings. The techniques of perspective were applied to the painting of the scenery which became of increasing importance as unspoken narration to the dialogue of the actors.

Penny readings.

The oral performance of literature entered a further development stage during the late nineteenth century. The Industrial Revolution of the late eighteenth century and continuing into the following century and the Victorian Age, brought new wealth and greater leisure opportunities for the middle classes. The social reforms in the latter half of the century had led to the growth of the middle class and a demand for social accomplishments which included reading. The ability to read well made one 'respectable and pleasing' (9) and there was a growing taste for culture and quality.

The recitation of literature as Penny Readings began as a popular movement during the late 1860's and continued until 1914. Any adult could gain experience in reading to an audience where the admission price to the public was one penny. Cox believed that those who could read should help those who could not read at all or "who read so imperfectly that reading is a laborious task" (10). The rules and illustrations on reading were not designed to instruct the reader in 'how to read', but to make *suggestions* for self-education in 'the art of reading'. Volunteer readers were to be advised that "Reading is an Art requiring education equally with the Art of Singing" (11).

The new 'Public Reading Society' (established *ca.* 1860) offered public readings "at the smallest charge" with the "office of reader to be gratuitously performed". These readings were to be seen not as formal instruction but as *entertainment*. Cox felt that "the excitement of a reader experience in arousing and sharing the emotions of an audience taught more about the art of reading in one evening than could be acquired in "twenty trials with none to hear". This was an early recognition of the significance and impact of the presence of an audience, and Cox advised that "Readers should survey the audience with polite attentiveness before beginning".

The 'smallest charge' was made because it was considered that "Free admission would downgrade the value of the performance". Various local venues were used for the readings, "Town Hall, vestry room or public school-room can always be obtained at no other expense than the candles for lighting it".

Twentieth century

The 'Great War' of 1914-1918 was a momentous social turning point with its significant impact on literature and the arts. Much of the formality of the Victorian and Edwardian ages was lost with the introduction of new social attitudes and behaviour.

A new form of 'verse speaking' was introduced in England around 1920. The purpose was "to gain literary appreciation through a new approach to the speaking of poetry". This was based on three principles – poetry should be written for the ear, not for the eye, the poem was more important than the personality of the reciter, and that poetry should be shared and enjoyed by many people (12)

A number of poetry festivals were held, with the strong influence of the poet John Masefield. Later, Masefield wished to eliminate the competitive element of the festivals and initiated a new way of writing "to suit the speaker". In 1928 some verse plays were 'acted out' on a simple dais with only a few chairs and with almost no action. Both Marjorie Gullen and Elsie Fogerty, well known teachers of speech, stressed the value of a beautiful voice and good speech as essentials in speaking poetry and that it must be seen as an art.

During the second half of the twentieth century there was a resurgence of interest in the public performance of poetry. As Josephine Johnson pointed out, in 1961 audiences in Liverpool were young, non-intellectual, working-class people in their twenties. "The poetry was loose, performed with less truth to language than truth to feeling" (13). This surging popular activity came to a head with the 1965 'Poetryfest' in the Royal Albert Hall, London, but this explosion of popular enthusiasm did not last. Later, Poetry Festivals began to be held during the seventies encouraged by the Poetry Society. Awards were made for performances and the chief expectations were for the speaker to communicate a "sensitivity to and awareness of the poet's intention, and to convey the individual voice of each chosen poet".

It may be debated whether any poetry or prose reading is enhanced by competitive reading. Each individual in the audience will have their own personal response to the performance and, while the receiving of an award may be a measurement of competence (in the view of a particular examiner) it cannot be a reflection of the effect of a performance on each individual listener. The performance of poetry has continued with varying degrees of enthusiasm into the twenty-first century, and the writing of poetry continues to blossom further. The English continue to discover that they "carry magic in the mouth, the great and special magic of English, an inheritance of poetry that craves to be performed" (14).

The twentieth century saw other important developments in 'literature in performance'. Two notable events occurred in America; a performance of an excerpt from Bernard Shaw's play *Man and Superman*, '*Don Juan in Hell*', and a production of Stephen Vincent Benét's epic poem *John Brown's Body*. The latter was an adaptation by Charles Laughton devised for three players and a chorus; it was performed at the New Century Theatre, New York in 1953, starring Judith Andersen, Raymond Massey and Tyrone Power. The production was acclaimed as an "outstanding Broadway Performance" and it then toured the continent to further acclaim and was revived in two later seasons, 1968-9 and 1971-2. These productions were not 'plays' in the conventional sense but were new and exciting presentations of 'literature in performance'. They were performed on a stage without scenery and with only a simple curtain back-drop.

Other noteworthy contributions to the New York stage from the U.K. included Terry Hand's *Pleasure and Repentance* and John Barton's *The Hollow Crown*. Staging for these productions was simple, five chairs arranged in a semi-circle around a table. Clive Barnes (New York Times, April 22 1974) commented "they really do present a different kind of theatre". After seeing a performance of *Sylvia Plath*, Barnes commented that "poetry is what drama is all about. It is the hard core of the dramatic experience – everything else is peripheral documentary" (15).

In America in the 1950s attention was being paid to the reading of prose works with the introduction of Readers Theatre within the field of education. The intention was to encourage young persons to read and enjoy books through reading aloud; this movement, and its other manifestations are explored next.

Notes.
1. Robert F. Sonkowsky, Oral Performance and Ancient Greek Literature, in *Performance of literature in historical perspective*, ed. D.W. Thompson (Lanham, MD, University Press of America, 1983), p.12.
2. Arthur Bryant, *Makers of the Realm*, (London, Collins, 1955), p.113.
3. Dwight Conquergood, *Literary and Oral performance in Anglo-Saxon England; conflict and confluence of traditions*, in Thompson, ibid, p.135.
4. Homer Pfandas, *The Popular sermon of the medieval friars in England*, (NY, New York University, 1932, p18-19).

5. Catherine Regan, *Liturgy and preaching as oral context for medieval English literature,* in *Performance of literature in historical perspective*, in Thompson, ibid, p.154.
6. Baldassare Castiglione, *The Courtier*, trans. T. Hoby, (London, David Nutt), 1900, p.69.
7. Steven Guazzo, *The Civile Conversation*, trans. G. Pettie and B. Young, (Constable, 1925) p.138.
8. Diane Bornstein, *Performing oral discourse as a form of sociability during the Renaissance,* in Thompson, ibid, p.217.
9. Quoted in www.imagination.com
10. Evelyn M. Sivier, *Penny Readings; popular elocution in late nineteenth century England.* 1983, in Thompson, ibid, p.154.
11. Edward W. Cox, *The Arts of reading, writing and speaking*, (London, Warne, 1881) p.180.
12. Evelyn M. Sivier, *English Poets, Teachers and Festivals in a "Golden Age of Poetry Speaking"*, 1920-1950, in Thompson, ibid, p283-4.
13. Josephine J. Johnson, *Return of the Scops; English poetry performance since 1961,* in Thompson, ibid. p.302.
14. Richard Church, *Verse speaking today*, in *Speech of our time*, ed. Clive Sansom, p136.
15. Clive Barnes, New York Times, January 17, 1974.

3. Contemporary Performance of Literature.

Readers Theatre.
The term Readers Theatre describes dramatic performances in which lines are read rather than memorized and at which an audience is normally present. It is the creative reading of any type of literature which contains 'theatre' whether as a play or otherwise. Originally this was used in the context of the classroom, but performances now embrace all imaginable venues – theatre, nursing home, living-room (drawing-room), street and field. Any type of literary work may provide suitable material for performance – literature, poetry, plays, musicals, magazines and newspapers. Much has been written on the subject and there are many expert teachers and practitioners.

The Readers Theatre movement appeared in the latter half of the twentieth century in the United States of America. Directed especially towards the classroom, the intention was to stimulate interest in books and reading among young students. Book texts were adapted and the children themselves read aloud to the audience. Stories were performed in the classroom as an introduction to books and drama in the form of simple theatrical performances.

Readers Theatre continues to be presented in North America but has undergone some significant changes evolving back into forms of amateur drama. The technique is still used primarily in classroom settings. The intention is to stimulate young people's interest in books and reading. The essential original focus was on the reading aloud of a written text. Although widely used in primary education it is now extended to teenagers and young adults.

However, low levels of proficiency in reading and writing persist in many western countries and young people need encouragement to read books and develop their imaginations. The continuing development of technology tends towards a lessened use of printed books and greater communication through digitally printed words and images.

The basic principles of Readers Theatre were to provide a creative stimulus for students to use their imagination and to interpret literary works in a classroom setting. It was also intended to promote an understanding with students and teachers that to see and hear literature performed in the classroom is as relevant to thoughtful educational development as it is to read literature silently. Readers Theatre is concerned with the 'inherent theatricality of literature', particularly with the dramatic role that sights, sounds or words can play in a classroom performer. The success of Readers Theatre depends on the skill of the performers, the selection of evocative literature, the creative use of space and the available rehearsal time.

The particular advantages were cited as the ease of production for performance as the text was read aloud and did not need to be memorized, and that no scenery, staging or lighting was required. Lois Walker comments that "like oral story-telling, readers theatre can create images by suggestion that could never be realistically portrayed on stage. Space and time can be shrunk or stretched, fantastic worlds can be created, marvellous journeys can be enacted. Readers Theatre frees the performers and the audiences from the physical limitations of conventional theatre, letting the imagination soar" (1). The costs of production are minimal but with a maximal enjoyment by the audience.

When Readers Theatre was introduced in America in the 1950s attention was being paid to the reading of prose works. The intention was to encourage young persons to read and enjoy books through reading aloud. One expert practitioner, Gerald Lee Ratliff, describes Readers Theatre as being concerned with "dramatic visualization" of literary texts and he believes that performers should be challenged vocally as well as physically in role-playing literary characters and attitudes (2). Other educationalists have explored these ideas and enthusiastic supporters have adapted a range of texts for performance.

Readers Theatre continues to evolve in its methods of presentation. Currently it now embraces memorization of the text together with enhanced staging devices using scenery, lighting and costumes with make-up; all of these are now apparently regarded as essential ingredients. The early simple classroom reading performances have become more ambitious and elaborate and may now include full dramatic staging and a proscenium arch to enhance the theatricality of the presentations. Technically Readers Theatre is still a form of 'literature in performance' but it appears to have merged back into the mainstream of amateur drama. As an educational tool it continues to have merit and is used variously in colleges and universities.

Theatre of the Mind (Imagination)

Another term used for 'literature in performance' is 'Theatre of the Mind' or 'Theatre of the Imagination'. Using this term, attention is drawn to the *method* of presentation. Performing in a small and intimate acting space there is no scenery, stage lighting or character costumes, all of which are conjured up in the minds and imaginations of the audience by the players. Here, in 'Theatre of the Imagination' the emphasis is on the skills of the performers to create location and character.

'Theatre of the Imagination' seems to be a particularly appropriate name that could be used comprehensively for the broad, generic, topic of 'literature in performance'. (In the early days the term used was 'Group Performance of Literature'.)

The essential elements emerge as,

1. A literary text, crafted by its original author, is performed by reading it aloud to an audience (some passages may be memorized and acted).
2. The audience comprises a small group of persons in an intimate venue (the social response).
3. The performers are restricted to a handful of players (appropriate to the playing space and the requirements of interpreting the text).
4. The story is brought to life through the performers' skills of interpretation in reading and acting, stimulating the imagination of the audience.

This is not the original form of Readers Theatre which is essentially performed with young persons, usually as a classroom event. Theatre of the Imagination is an alternative and more general term which draws particular attention to the intimacy of the performances and the role of the audience; here the performance focuses on the simplicity of the presentation and the impact of the each individual present. Using an original written text it brings both classic and modern works of prose and poetry to life that would not be viable in conventional theatre.

There is an ancient Chinese saying, *"Tell me, I forget", Show me, I remember, Involve me, and I understand"*. In Theatre of the Imagination each member of the audience is drawn into the performance and is involved in a more intimate way than happens in a larger auditorium. A conventional 'play' is performed on a stage behind an invisible 'glass wall' separating actors and audience and where the audience become essentially observers, watching the action unfold and with occasional encouragement (or sometimes disapproval). With the intimacy of Theatre of the Imagination the performance is shared with the audience in a more direct way without any separation. The audience becomes involved in the presentation. This suggests that this form of theatre can lead to an understanding of the work that is different from viewing a play in a conventional theatre. It is this factor that lies behind its teaching use in university departments. Professor Evelyn Vitz has employed these techniques in her courses on Medieval French; a student describes the impact of performance as that "it breathes life into the text"; "performing, rather than simply reading a text, allows hearers to experience a medieval work in something like the original reception context" (3). Performing a text encourages audience (listener) involvement and that involvement leads to greater understanding of the text. For a student (or a player) the act of performing concentrates the mind and makes the text more memorable. This is an important factor in teaching and learning and is one reason why performance is used in universities and schools; it can be a powerful educational tool. For the audience the intimacy of the shared experience creates a sense of involvement in the story and its performance that leads to a particular impact of understanding and emotional response.

Neuro-scientists have shown that we learn more from whatever has emotional context for us; this is a function of the limbic brain. The emotional impact of being amongst a small group in intimate surroundings can be particularly personal which differs somewhat from being present in a larger auditorium. An early example of an intimate performance was seen when Chaucer read his *Canterbury Tales* to his friends and fellow guests; his stories of contemporary people with all their failings and beliefs clearly had impact and popularity. Almost all medieval vernacular works were originally intended for live performance of some kind with its appeal to the emotions; private reading was rare and silent reading was virtually non-existent. Today, the presentation of contemporary 'chamber theatre' has similar impact.

Watching a conventional stage play requires input from the mind of each member of the audience ('the audience response'). The scenery and lighting 'set the scene' from the opening, the costumes provide the time-set and indicate the characters, and the actors bring the characters to life in believable personalities and situations. Together these are the equivalent of the author's narration in a prose story. On the stage all this 'visual narration' is then interpreted from the individual viewer's personal knowledge and experience. In a darkened auditorium, surrounded by several hundred like-minded people, competent actors can move an audience to laughter or to tears in a moving and emotional occasion drawing on a social consensus of understanding. When the house lights go up at the end of the performance each person returns to a personal normality fairly quickly without a great deal, if any, interaction with others leaving the theatre.

In contrast with the conventional theatre, the closeness and intimacy of a performance of Theatre of the Imagination, and the familiarity of eye contact with the performers bond actors and audience together in a particularly involved way. This is shared theatre and becomes a specially intimate and personal experience for each person. The narrative of the performance has a special, and different, meaning for each individual present. An alternative term used for this method of performance is 'Chamber Theatre' or 'Drawing-room Theatre'.

Chamber Theatre (Drawing-room theatre)

According to Wikipedia, "Chamber Theatre is a method of adapting literary works to the stage using a maximal amount of the work's original text and often minimal and suggestive settings. In Chamber Theatre narration is included in the performed text and the narrator may be played by multiple actors". This definition could be applied equally to Readers Theatre and does not adequately distinguish Chamber Theatre as a specific form of 'literature in performance'.

A particular and defining feature of Chamber Theatre is that it is a form of theatre performed by a small number of players, typically 2-4, in a small and usually intimate venue such as a private drawing-room. This echoes the term used in the world of music; 'chamber music' describes a performance by 2-8 musicians and presented in a small concert room before a correspondingly small number of people in the audience. In contrast 'conventional theatre' is performed on a larger scale and corresponds to 'orchestral music' which is performed by a large group of musicians (the orchestra) in a public concert hall.

The emphasis in Chamber Theatre is on the size of the audience and the number of players; both of these factors contribute to the intimacy of the occasion. The number of players may be between two and four and the audience might average around thirty persons. However the number of players will be influenced by the requirements of the work being performed and by the venue itself. Narration is combined with dialogue and shared by the players and thus the gender and age of the players become less relevant than when 'casting' a conventional play. In a chamber theatre performance there is always a marked intimacy between players and audience with direct eye contact and rapport expressed in gesture and manner of reading and speaking. It is these characteristics that are the distinguishing features of chamber theatre.

26

Marc Horwitz, an actor with the Performance Workshop Theatre in Baltimore, U.S.A., describes chamber theatre as a distinctly different form of stagecraft; "In this environment an actor can explore different parts of the voice – a lower pitch, a softer tone. Here the slightest change in breathing, the smallest gesture, even in posture, are tremendously important in a way they aren't in a normal theatre". The Director, Marlyn Robinson comments that "The actors are so close to the audience that it's like the close-ups in film. Actors can act with their faces in a way they never could in a larger theatre" (4). The small theatre represents not just a difference in size but also a difference in kind.

This intimacy, and the closer relationship between performers and audience, enables a different and a more detailed interpretation of the performance than is usual in a larger auditorium. This can lead to a more personal impact on understanding and enjoyment of the performed work. Today's Chamber Theatre may be regarded as a reflection of medieval story-telling seen in the manner of Chaucer's reading of his *Canterbury Tales* to friends and guests in his Host's chamber. When the *Tales* are presented in this way in a modern drawing-room we come close to an authentic 'Chaucer Experience'.

Presenting chamber theatre.
A chamber theatre presentation differs from a conventional stage play in both the intention and the process. The underlying intention is to bring a literary work (prose, fiction or poetry) to life through the act of performance. The literary work itself has been crafted by the original author to tell a story in a particular way using specifically chosen words and phrases. This is not unlike the work of a Director of a stage play who reads the script, decides a possible course of action for presentation and then encourages the actors to bring their own interpretations of character to develop the story.

The process in chamber theatre is to discover, as far as possible, the intentions of the author and the meaning of the words used, and then to tell the story using the original words of the author through narration and performance. The inclusion of narration into the performance enables the players to take an objective view of the story-line. The players are not acting solely as individual characters, as in a stage play, but they are an integrated group of narrators and actors; they share a responsibility with the Director to understand the work to a level that is not always seen with amateur actors in a stage play.

It is this responsibility that enables and guides chamber theatre players to share that knowledge and understanding of the work with the audience. They do not 'talk amongst themselves' in front of the listeners, instead, these players are presenting the story as a shared performance with the listeners.

This, in turn, requires active co-operation from the listeners. The audience is not a body of spectators, watchers who are hearing words and enjoying the story movement; in chamber theatre each individual in the audience listens and observes and each participates at a different level to the members of a conventional theatre audience.

Two important factors become apparent in this form of theatre. The players presenting chamber theatre need a high level of competency in communicating with the audience which includes both verbal and non-verbal communication skills. The small number of players involved and the intensity of the rehearsals will enable development of these skills. The other significant factor of chamber theatre is the small size of the audience and the proximity of the individuals to each other in intimate surroundings. This creates a particular sense of belonging to the performance that is difficult to produce in this way with the audience in a large auditorium.

The audience factor is further enhanced by the fact that those present at a chamber theatre performance are the guests invited by the Host and are likely to be known to each other or share a common interest. This factor helps to establish a sense of togetherness from the very beginning.

Chamber Theatre and the Chaucer Experience.
An early manifestation of chamber theatre is seen with Chaucer in medieval England. Today, presenting *The Canterbury Tales* as contemporary chamber theatre reflects the way that Chaucer would have originally read his stories to friends and guests. Such presentations in a drawing-room environment come close to an authentic 'Chaucer Experience' which is lost when the *Tales* are performed in a stage play format. Performing the words aloud in the intimacy of a modern day drawing-room (the equivalent of a medieval 'chamber') brings the stories to life in a personal way that is different from watching a play. Hearing the *Tales* in this way is the closest experience one can share with Chaucer's audiences as they heard the stories for the first time.

A number of *The Canterbury Tales* have been arranged and presented in this way as chamber theatre. This performance experience has led to a different viewpoint on the presentation and impact of the *Tales*. A single narrator simulating Chaucer's own reading of his work, can be seen as an interesting historical re-enactment.

It is possible, perhaps even likely, that following Chaucer's death (1400) several of his supporters would have continued to read the Tales aloud as entertainment. A reading by two presenters has a different impact on the listeners than from a single narrator. The event becomes a performance and very much a shared experience in the intimacy of 'chamber theatre'.

The experience of the modern arrangements for three players has been seen to be particularly effective with a preferred presentation grouping of two women and one man. The *Tales* may be presented as a single item or in groups of two or three *Tales* which may be the way that Chaucer himself would have read them on each occasion.

Although some purists may consider the use of the original Middle English text to be truly 'authentic', there is no consensus of agreement amongst the scholars as to the 'correct' pronunciation to be used. Thus reading the Middle English text aloud as a form of public entertainment can be seen as a form of antiquarianism and the contemporary impact of Chaucer's stories is lost. Scholars continue to debate the phonology of Middle English with a legitimate aim to assist students and teachers towards an understanding of the texts.

Such focus on the original Chaucer text tends to overlook the literary value of his work and obscures the opportunity of the general public to enjoy the *Tales* in relation to contemporary social behaviour. It is thus recommended that Chaucer's intention and practice should be followed by presenting the *Tales* in the familiar (vernacular) language of the audience. This makes for easier understanding of the stories which is the primary intention of the presentation.

There is little doubt that in Chaucer's day his word portraits of contemporary characters would have been widely recognised and understood; in particular there was a shared general dislike of Summoners and Pardoners. Religion and the Church were dominant influences throughout the medieval period and permeated people's lives at every level. Although the social organisation has changed, it is remarkable how little has changed in human behaviour; the characters and their actions are as relevant today as they were six hundred years ago.

Little is known of how these stories became so widely known and loved, but in medieval society mixed assemblies ate and conversed together under one roof. In some households there would have been a resident reader and the occasional itinerant entertainer would bring news and other story-telling. Music, singing and reading aloud were the norm for entertainment and literacy was limited. In these daily communal gatherings a reader needed to attract and hold attention above the general household noise. There is an illustration of Chaucer apparently reading his work at the Court of Richard II but it is not known if this was a unique occasion. It is assumed that Chaucer would have entertained his Hosts and fellow guests by reading some of the Tales on occasions, but we do not know in what other ways the *Tales* became known.

The *General Prologue* to *The Canterbury Tales* was written in 1386 and Chaucer died in 1400; this is a very short time-scale for the Tales to have become so well-known and admired. It can be presumed that some of Chaucer's friends would have had copies made, and indeed, some eighty copies or fragments are known, but copying a text was expensive and a slow and laborious process. It is likely that some enthusiasts would have used such texts and would have copied Chaucer's practice to read the *Tales* aloud at social gatherings.

Some seventy years after Chaucer's death the printing press was brought to England. The second book to be printed was Chaucer's *Canterbury Tales*. In that short time the *Tales* had become so widely popular that William Caxton, the printer, decided to print this work as the second title for publication. Without any widespread promotion of the *Tales* by the author in his lifetime and the limited manual copying of the text, it is reasonable to suppose that others, friends and supporters, would have continued Chaucer's practice of reading the *Tales* as entertainment. The surviving professional entertainers of the period are also likely to have performed the *Tales*. It may be speculated that as the number of professional entertainers was declining some of them might have added the *Tales* to their own travelling repertoire. Copyright and plagiarism were not an issue in those days and authors borrowed ideas from others freely.

What is certain is that by 1477, when William Caxton brought his printing-press to London, *The Canterbury Tales* were widely known. Once the work had been printed and distributed it was possible for many more people to have copies although the limited state of literacy would have restricted personal and silent reading. In those early social events where *The Canterbury Tales* were read aloud we may see the elements of present-day 'chamber theatre'.

The English theatre.
The development of popular story-telling followed a new course with the emerging 'commercial' theatre of the later medieval period. The Church had used drama in its teaching and had sponsored performances of the 'Mystery' and 'Miracle' plays. Later these were moved out to the village square and merged into elaborate pageants and spectacles which were sponsored by the various medieval craft guilds and performed by their members. In due course, places of entertainment moved into inn yards and later became theatres. Tudor England saw the building of several purpose-built theatres in London including the Swan, the Rose and the Globe theatres. Plays were also written for, and performed in schools by boy actors, e.g. *Ralph Roister Doister*, by Nicholas Udall. Later, in Shakespeare's day these open-air stages began to be roofed over and thereafter modern theatre with indoor lighting began to evolve.

Other changes were taking place. From the London dialect of Middle English spoken by Chaucer, modern English emerged as the common language of the people and the giants of literature strode forth, Marlowe, Jonson and Shakespeare. This flowering of the English theatre continued to evolve through the succeeding years with the introduction and development of technical theatre (proscenium, scenery and lighting) and on to the experimentation in the twentieth century including a return to open thrust stages and the constant re-interpretation of plays and characters. In all these changes the popular amateur drama has continued to thrive and develop alongside the professional theatre.

The conventional stage play.
Whether or not reading aloud as a performance may be considered as 'acting' is a matter of opinion. The reader-player is concerned to interpret the text, the characters and the story-line in a similar way to the stage actor. The latter immerses himself into a specific character role acting out in real-time the words and actions of the character and performing behind the invisible 'glass wall' separating the players and the audience. The reader-player sits on the audience side of the story combining narration with the dialogue between the characters. This requires an adroit performance which appears to be equally, or possibly more complex, than that of the conventional stage actor.

In a conventional play the actors are cast as individual characters created by the playwright to tell a story which is set out in the play script. They learn their 'lines', the speeches allocated to each character, and they begin to discover each character role in terms of personality and motivation of action combining the voice, gestures and movements which are considered to be appropriate to the character. Various techniques have been devised to accomplish this aim by actors and directors, notably 'naturalistic acting' introduced by Stanislavsky. Among many amateur actors, those without training in professional techniques, this is largely an intuitive process based on the individual's personal experience of life and relationships. There are many such actors who have outstanding intuitive skills of acting and reach levels of interpretation comparable to many trained professionals.

At the rehearsal stage in front of an audience of one, the Director, the actors explore ways to perform the story in the script. By repeated rehearsal, words and actions are integrated into coherent and meaningful action. In performance the actors talk amongst themselves, aiming to live out the story on stage as though it were real life and actually happening for the first time. When the director of the play is satisfied that a reasonable level of performance has been attained, the play is put before a general audience.

Now the rehearsal actions are repeated, but this time with 'outsiders', the public audience, looking in at the action on the stage. The actors continue to talk amongst themselves but they are behind an invisible wall which separates them from the onlookers. This relationship is maintained even with a thrust stage or a performance 'in-the-round'. However close the actors are to the audience there is still a separation, a demarcation, between the actors performing the story and those who watch from 'outside'. For the most part the actors act out the story-line as though the audience was not present except that the volume of speech is adjusted to the size of the theatre and the words and actions are 'projected', out to the far corners of the auditorium. The continuous action of the story may be temporarily halted by the audience response of applause or laughter.

The intimate performance.
The performance of literature through a shared reading of the work as in chamber theatre is different from a conventional 'acted play' as described above. The former is essentially an act of sharing the work between players and audience based on the stimulation of imagination and is a particularly intimate form of performance. The conventional play is performed before an audience who are looking in at the story from outside the 'real time' of the actors. In addition to the actors' dialogue, the Director has provided 'narration' in the form of scenery and setting to further assist an understanding of the story.

The use of voice and body to interpret the text are similar for the conventional actor and the reader-player; the one particular difference can be seen in the nature of the relationship with the audience. In the small venues of chamber theatre each member of the audience is within social distance of the players and voice and gestures do not need to be 'projected'; instead the closeness and direct eye contact creates an intimate event where the audience is drawn into the performance and become personally involved. The story-telling is presented in the 'real time' of the audience and the players. Some features of the shared and intimate performance are described in the following chapters.

In the United States both Readers Theatre and Chamber Theatre are performed to small and large size audiences; often the players perform on a raised platform or stage for better visibility and include stage lighting. This enables larger audiences but loses out on the intimacy of the presentation. As described here, Chamber Theatre is essentially intimate theatre where the story is shared by the players with the audience and the size of the audience is significant. By sharing the same space, the players and the audience form a social relationship which is absent in a larger auditorium. It is this intimacy which enhances the performance (the players' interpretation of the text) and the emotional response and understanding by the audience.

Notes.
1. Lois Walker, www.Scripts for schools.com
2. Gerald Lee Ratcliff, *Introduction to Readers Theatre; a guide to classroom performance.* (Colorado Springs, CO, Meriwether 1999), p.4.
3. Evelyn Bauer Vitz, *Teaching Arthur through performance*, (Arthuriana 15, 2005).
4. Marc Horwitz, www.performancetheatreworkshop.org.

Part Two: Preparation and Performance.

4. Performance and Interpretation.

Communication and performance.
Communication between individuals may take different forms and have different purposes. It may be oral, written or non-verbal communication with the purpose of a command or a request, or the transfer of ideas or feelings through statements or questions. When an oral story-teller performs there is an informal communication of a connected set of ideas as entertainment or edification for the audience. When this oral communication becomes focussed in a written text the process tends to be more formal than when using the spoken word. The act of reading a written text aloud becomes a process of balance between oral familiarity and the formality of a written text; this is the act of interpretation. Beverly Whitaker considered that 'interpretation' is best defined as "the study of literature through performance" (1).

The first stage in the process of communicating and interpreting a written text through speech requires some understanding of the work. The techniques of literary analysis and criticism are applied to explore the meaning of a text and this process can provide valuable and productive insight into a literary work. Those techniques can be found in the many books on literary analysis and will not be detailed here.

Several factors are involved in this process of interpretation through performance. A performance is influenced by the number and quality of the performers, the size and nature of the audience, and the environment where the story is performed. A performance to young people will be different in vocabulary and style of presentation than it would be when performing to an adult and mature audience. The latter group will have different and wider experience with which to interpret the words and actions of the performers. A performance given in an intimate private drawing-room can have a different character than one given in a public library meetings room.

Before one gets too serious about drama, acting and performance, it may be useful to remember that Brecht believed that the business of theatre is entertainment and needs no other justification than being fun. However, this is not a matter of just 'playing around' on the stage; entertainment is a skill which requires discipline and dedication to acquire and develop technique. In order to become a good performer one does need to work hard at having fun.

Here we are considering entertainment as crafted story-telling where the written words are interpreted through performance. The act of 'performing' by reading the text aloud to an audience, involves interpreting the words used with attention to the author's style and the punctuation employed together with non-verbal gestures made by the performer. This act of interpretation is influenced by the background knowledge and the life experience of the performer and together creates a meaningful event, or as Professor Evelyn Vitz describes it, "breathes life into the text". By 'performance' we imply that the text has been read, analysed and prepared for interpretation before it is presented to an audience.

The preparation for performance may begin with an exploration to understand the author of the story, delving into the personal background, circumstances and intentions behind the creation of the work. The text itself is explored in some depth for guidance on how the story may be communicated and interpreted. The author's vocabulary and the way the words are selected and used become significant factors towards interpretation. A performed text is influenced by the author's choice of words, phrasing and use of punctuation; together, these form a guide to the spoken presentation and is similar to musical notation which guides a musician on the way the notes in a composition are to be played – their pitch, duration and volume. The story-telling performance may be an interpretation by a single performer alone, or it may be a joint effort by a group of players with the help of a director, much as the conductor of an orchestra and the musicians create a consensus of sound to perform a musical composition. The crafted story-teller, using words instead of musical notes, is similarly concerned with pitch, pace and pause.

Words are the foundation blocks of performance and are the particular crafted elements of story-telling which need to be understood and explored as a basis for interpretation. In a story, words are linked in sentences which are governed by rules of grammar and syntax but are modified by the author's style and manner of writing. Words can have different meanings in differing circumstances. In creating a story an author chooses specific words to convey particular meaning and effect although such words may have different interpretations for the performer and for the individuals in the audience. Each person interprets words they read or hear according to a general cultural understanding but this will also be modified by their own personal knowledge and background experience.

Thus the performer needs to try to appreciate what the author intends (literary analysis) and then to interpret the words and sentences from a personal point of view. Ultimately, however clearly conveyed, the final interpretation and understanding of a performance lies with the personal knowledge and understanding of each individual in the audience of the words heard and the actions they observe of the players. Some appreciation of the nature of the audience will be helpful to the performer as communicator.

The analysis of a literary text begins with questions about the author as well as the text itself. Who is, or was, the author? Relevant questions may relate to age, gender, nationality and domicile. Within the text one can look for the general style of writing and possible external influences on the author's thinking. Themes and symbolisms can be explored. Other aspects to be explored include the vocabulary, phrasing, and figures of speech used. The way these are handled by the author will be important in characterisation within the story and also in its setting. (Consider the opening lines of some well-known classic stories, for example, Jane Austen's *Pride and Prejudice*, Charles Dickens' *A Tale of Two Cities*, or *Under Milk Wood* by Dylan Thomas; in each case the first sentence 'sets the scene' of the work vividly in a few evocative words.)

Both Cicely Berry and Patsy Rodenburg draw attention to the power of words. The player (reader) needs to 'own words'; knowledge of a word changes as we experience life, and its meaning will change for each one of us through our personal development. By 'owning words' in this way the player moves from the intellectual knowledge of a text to a deeper sensual and emotional understanding – "Words begin to grow roots in the heart and soul". Rodenburg explains this, "What I always think is that there is somebody out there in the audience who understands the experience of my character (words) better than I do. Give them the words and they can have that experience" (2).

Although these remarks apply both to prose and poetry, the 'performance' of a poem involves more than an understanding of the author's intentions in creating it. Feelings and emotions are engendered by the words and rhythms used; the performer opens an empathy with the hearer of which only the individual hearer is aware. Performed poetry is a presentation of human drama with many complex overtones of emotions and meanings; some aspects of this are discussed in a later chapter.

Imagination.

All story-telling is created with imagination. Imagination has been described as 'the intelligent prediction of future events based on a sensitive understanding and perceptive analysis of the past'. By re-arranging the known we can create the inner experience of the unknown; this is the province of imagination. Freud traces imaginative activity back to the child who is consumed by the best-loved and most absorbing occupation, play.

The 'silent reader' (of a story) creates/reconstructs the story using his/her own imaginative experience. This also occurs with the reader of a play-script who reads the text with "an imaginative construction of theatre audiences" (3). Such 'imaginative construction' is based almost exclusively on the clues provided in the text (4).

In a conventional theatre setting the actors' and the director's understanding of the text together with the intentions of the author create a visual three-dimensional experience. When performing literature similar 'sound images' are created from the text but the individuals in the audience are required to respond and to 'interpret' these images for themselves (Theatre of the Imagination). On the conventional stage, the actors interact with each other and interpret words within their own 'real world' which may be quite different from the actual worlds of individuals in the audience, e.g. Shakespeare's *King Lear*.

This 'image response' is conveyed through the dialogue – what is said (words used) and how it is said (voice inflection and including facial expression and gestures). As Berry points out, each individual reacts and interprets what is heard from a personal point of view. Each performer works from within himself to 'act out' or interpret a specific character; this process of acting has been described as *the imaginative communication of significant experience*.

Jane Goodall, from her extensive research with the primates, has observed that "imagination, not tool-making or feeling for another, is what separates us from other primates". This has been echoed by Albert Einstein, "imagination is more important than knowledge". Limited actual experience requires extensive development of the imagination. Throughout history man has continually asked "*What if*"? and has then suggested possible answers.

In a crafted story-telling performance the players use the author's words to strike chords in the imaginations of the audience. Words and phrases create images which the individual listener can echo from personal experience. There may be a general consensus of understanding about the story plot (though not always), but each hearer will 'see' locations and characters from their own personal point of view. In this way imagination becomes a way of personal visualization and applies meaning accordingly. It has been said that 'the more we rely on imagination the more we grow as flexible and mature personalities'. The intimate performance of chamber theatre as 'Theatre of the Imagination' can stimulate imaginative responses in the audience in a particularly powerful and personal way.

For years most theatre acting in Western Europe has taken place in front of an audience separated from each other by an invisible wall where the members of the audience are essentially watching the story from the outside. During the twentieth century the stage (the acting area) moved out into the auditorium in an effort to place the action closer to the audience; yet the invisible wall remained. Even with the extreme arrangement of theatre in-the-round the 'wall' persists, but here it encloses the action on all sides. The audience is closer to the action but is still separated and outside the space where the actors perform.

The wall separating performers and audience dissolves in the performance of chamber theatre; performers and audience share the same space and there is direct eye contact between them. The 'story' of the play is no longer confined to the actors' character dialogue; the thoughts and words of the characters in the 'story' are combined with spoken narration and are directly shared with the individuals in the audience.

In the efforts to bring the action closer to the audience the traditional proscenium arch theatre has evolved towards variations of the thrust stage, reaching out to the audience. In this respect the modern stage echoes the seventeenth century acting areas as seen in the 'Great Globe'. This evolution has been accompanied by the use of technology in lighting and scenic effects; the opening ceremonies of the 2012 Olympic and Paralympic Games in London demonstrated this spectacular use of three-dimensional technology. The audience remains, and even more so, as spectators. The high costs of this technology lead inevitably to larger auditoria and larger audiences paying higher admission fees to pay for it all. Another example is the new theatre of the Royal Shakespeare Company in Stratford upon Avon.

Such elaborate spectacle tends to over-shadow the imaginations of the individuals in the audience; this was seen in the Royal Ballet's production of *Alice in Wonderland* (2012) which emphasised the 'voyeuristic' role of the audience. Elaborate image devices were used to illustrate characters and events within the story. This is far removed from a simple reading aloud of the story as written by Lewis Carroll where the words are intended to stimulate the listener's imaginations to visualize the story in an individual and personal way. Imaginative performances in small spaces are less expensive than staging in vast arenas but they can have great personal impact on participating individuals in the audience. The mantra 'small is beautiful' is relevant to chamber theatre and is a counter-balance to the increasing technological voyeurism of much twenty-first century theatre and spectacle.

Stephen Joseph has argued for more small audience theatre spaces "The phenomenon of theatre consists of a relatively small group of people (the actors) who act out the events of a story to the entertainment of a much larger group of people (the audience). The larger group, though, must not be so large that some members of the audience cannot see or hear properly" (5).

However, it is to be remembered that the 'theatre' is a reflection of life as lived by people; people change, life changes and 'theatre' changes – in the style of acting, the form of the buildings and manner of presentation. The theatre as a microcosm of specific life events deals with time, and is subject to time's changes. As an activity, theatre has continued through thousands of years in a particular form of story-telling – a performance of words and action to touch the imaginations of the listeners.

Memory.
An actor combines imagination with memory. The interpretation of a play (story) text starts with the actor's own memory to begin to understand place and character, the location of the story and the people involved. Some visualization from a past experience triggers a new image suggested by the author's words and this is then developed through a "What if?" process. The actor's memory will influence the delivery of words and any associated actions; the way some words are inflected, by tone, pitch and volume, may be drawn from the actor's subliminal memory.

Another form of memory relates to physical activity. The successful actor is likely to have a wide experience of life, personally and by observation of others. Extensive reading will further contribute to understanding people, situations and activities. All these become embedded in the actor's memory bank of life. This includes 'body memory' that essential part of life which enables a human being to function with a minimum of conscious thought. We rely on the inbuilt memories of actions we have learned, such as walking, opening a door, sitting on a chair, running a shower or drinking a cup of tea. Such body memory actions are combined with the player's imagination to create a character or a role. Using body memory lessens the effort of intellectual thought; the way a young actor can create the image of an older person, modifying his own body memory through observation of other people.

A creative actor must be observant to see how people behave in the basic acts of standing, walking and sitting. To these images are added conventional gestures and voice inflections. In this way the actor triggers imaginative visualizations in the audience and develops character and action from shared memories with the audience. In all performance, whether on a conventional stage or in the intimacy of chamber theatre, imagination and memory, together, are seen as the basic elements in performing.

The audience.
The performance of a text, whether as a story, poem or a play, requires an audience. However, defining the 'audience' inevitably involves value judgements. The word is derived from the Latin '*audio*', to hear or understand, which suggests a listening rather than a visual role. So are the individuals in an audience, listeners, viewers, witnesses, or are they accomplices or participants? Undoubtedly the audience is a mix of gender, age, social position, education and occupation as well as national identity, language and beliefs. Each individual will hear, see and interpret the words and action differently based on culture, education and personal experience. The understanding of the performance then becomes a shared interpretation of what is seen and heard rather than a detailed analysis of what the author wrote or intended.

Susan Bennett pointed to the "possibility that the response of the audience may influence the delivery of the performers, the live presence of spectators and performers in shared time and space" (6). The intimacy of a chamber theatre performance demonstrates the profound difference between the private reading of a book and the experience of attending a performance. Each individual in the audience is a participant with a personal interpretation of what is seen and heard. That response has an impact on the players and their performance which may be more immediate and have greater impact in the intimacy of the chamber theatre than might be experienced with a performance in a conventional theatre auditorium.

In performance mode words can be presented, as in music, using a range of interpretive devices; these include voice inflection, the way the words are spoken, and also the pauses and silences between words. This may be accompanied by non-verbal communication through body posture, position, movement and gesture. These elements will be considered in turn.

Performing with words.

The way we speak words, singly or in sentences, influences their interpretation. The manner of speaking involves voice inflection and includes tonality, pitch, volume and pace. Underlying these factors is the attitude of the speaker and the circumstances of speaking. The old adage is relevant, 'It's not what you say, but how you say it that is important'. Nic Sebastian has explained that "Voice is sense, an organ of investigation just like fingers, ears, tongue, eyes or nose. Voice brings you information not otherwise available to you" (7).

The primary rule of communication in performance mode is to speak clearly. Good, clear speech commands attention and can be understood. The professional actor spends much time learning and practising how to stand, breathe and to speak clearly. Everyone who aims to read aloud in performance to others needs to do likewise.

Creating words (Breath and Breathing).

Speech is a coherent grouping of words, or the making of sounds with meaning. The human voice creates these sounds by the passage of air through the vocal cords in the larynx, the 'air tube' that lies in front of the 'food tube' (the oesophagus) passing through the neck. The 'air tube' is vital to life – without air we quickly die – but normal breathing is automatic, we don't need consciously to think about how to do it.

We do have to think about speech, about making words.

Breathing is a function of the diaphragm and ribs. The diaphragm forms the muscular floor of the chest cavity. As the diaphragm moves downward the ribs move outwards and breath is drawn into the lungs. Then, as the diaphragm relaxes it moves upwards and air is expelled from the lungs. This automatic action is aided by contraction of the abdominal and pelvic muscles.

Conscious sound, including words, is created by the passage of air through the vocal cords situated in the larynx. It is important that this airway through the larynx is kept clear and flexible in order to produce clear and full sounds. Several factors are involved to ensure this.

The head and neck must be aligned without tension. (Rotating the head first clockwise and then in an anti-clockwise direction is a useful preparatory exercise used by actors to release tension in the neck and throat before going on stage.) Support for the head and neck is provided by the muscles of the shoulders and the upper spine. The shoulders should be slightly dropped and relaxed with the natural support of the back and pelvic muscles. When in a standing posture the pelvis should lie flat, not tilted forwards, with the weight of the body supported through thigh, knee, heel and foot. The feet should be turned slightly outwards.

With the whole body in the full support mode voice production becomes controllable. It is important for every actor to understand the process of breathing and the significance of the body muscles to enable this support mode. (A detailed account of this body support and good voice production will be found in Barbara Houseman's excellent advice to actors, *Finding your voice*, and see also the guidance by Cicely Berry in her book *Voice and the actor*.)

Your voice is you.
Your voice is an important expression of your personality and you should feel comfortable with it without any forcing. This does not mean that you cannot, or should not, change the way you speak. Anyone who has played a wind instrument – flute, clarinet, recorder or trombone – will know that creating a musical tone goes beyond making the correct notes; controlling the air flow is the means to producing a quality tone. Listen to your voice, and to others speaking, and decide whether you might wish to make any changes in pitch, tone or volume in your speaking voice. Soft speakers may not always be heard clearly and a loud speaker may be considered to be over-bearing. A low pitch is often regarded as appropriate for a man. A very high pitched female voice can be too strident for some listeners. The quality of your voice can be an indication of your personality and how others see you.

Regional accents or slight speech impediments are the natural 'you'; there is no need to try to alter these. However, it should be recognised that a very pronounced regional accent may not be easily understood outside your own area.

Your voice is your personal instrument of expression and the means of communication with others and you should aim to be skilful in using it. If you played a musical instrument seriously you would expect to practise several hours every day; similar practice and dedication is needed to master your personal vocal instrument. To achieve competency in your speaking voice the advice is straightforward in three simple words – practise, practise, practise! Do not be content to read a text fluently and satisfactorily to yourself. Explore as many possibilities as you can for its interpretation and always do this with an audience present. This advice may seem strange, but performance requires an audience, you are not reading solely for your own amusement. Your practice audience might well be a stuffed animal (more consistent than a live one), but it is a valuable focus of attention and concentration.

Remember 'Murphy's Law', "When reading aloud you need to speak more slowly than you speak". Slowing down will enable you to create more expression and meaning into your words. In public performance your natural adrenaline will prevent any descent into being slow and boring.

Get involved with the ideas in the text and identify with them – this is your dramatic involvement. This must be natural and convincing to your listeners, unless you are trying deliberately to be ironic. You will need to 'come alive' with your words and feel involved with your reading. If you are not sincere and excited you cannot expect your audience to be excited and receptive.

Tell the story with your face, read with a smile for the most part and indicate clearly any sadness or despair; be firm and explicit with your anger or frustration. Show all this interest in your eyes and your posture.

Speaking practice.
Cultivate clarity in speaking and do not mumble or swallow words; do not let your words just die away. You may need to exaggerate mouth and lip movements; practising 'tongue twisters' can be helpful for precise articulation of sounds and words (see the Appendix for some suggestions). Some repetitive sounding of consonants and vowels can be helpful; enunciate similar sounding pairs, P and B, F and V, M and N, T and D. Pay attention to final sounded consonants and syllables which should not be 'dropped'; maintain the air flow through to the end of the sound. In normal speech there is often a tendency to gloss over and not give full value to a final '-ed' syllable. A final '-ing' syllable is also likely to be dropped. The following examples can be used for speaking practice; start by speaking each one slowly and enunciating each syllable clearly. Then increase the pace to your normal rate of speaking.

Wanted, waited, wilted.
Lasted longer than expected.
Melted into wasted moments.

Wanting, waiting, willing.
Longing and hoping.
Singing and dancing.

I am going to do it.
Does he want to do it?
Do you hope to do it?

Not such a bad thing.
A really red rose.
Hit it with a hammer.

Come and sit here.
Go and get the tea.
Just waiting and wanting to sing.

Last thing to do.
Best time to see it.
Wait in the West wing.

You and I and everyone.
Live and let live to the last.
Dust to dust and east to west.

I meant to dust the bedroom.
Panting and breathing fast.
Step up to the platform.

Be careful not to break the bottle.
Put the paint pot on the table.
You must not touch that chair.

A chamber theatre performance is an intimate event and a conversational way of speaking is appropriate. Introduce variety with variations in pitch, pace or volume of speaking. If you speak with your face and gestures your voice will be integrated intuitively and you will create a memorable performance. The practice suggestions in the following pages are intended to help stimulate your imagination and develop your communication skills.

Notes.

1. Beverly Whitaker, *Research Directions in the Performance of Literature*, Speech Monographs 40 August 1973, p.239.
2. Patsy Rodenburg, *The Actor speaks,*(London, Methuen, 1997), p.221.
3. Susan Wise Bauer, *The Well-trained Mind*, (New York, NY, Norton, 1999).
4. Kenneth Krauss, *Private Readings/public texts; playreaders' constructs of theatre audiences.* (Associated University Press, 1983), p.16.
5. Stephen Joseph, Theatre in the Round. (London, Barrie & Rockcliff, 1967), pp.9-10.
6. Susan Bennett, *The Role of the Theatre Audience: a Theory of Production and Reception* (Diss. McMaster University, 1988).
7. Nic Sebastian, www.verylikeawhale.wordpress.com.

5. The Speaking Voice

The human voice is a powerful tool for communicating intentions and ideas. Musical instruments can convey a wide range of feelings and emotions, creating sensations which 'strike a chord' within us, but the human voice is unique in its precision in communicating ideas, questions and instructions. Even a single word can be spoken in many different ways to indicate different meanings (this will be explored later). We begin by describing the principal elements of speech.

Tonality.
Tonality describes the character and quality of sound; this includes the register or range of the human voice. It may be referred to as 'euphony' which can be defined as an agreeable sound, the smoothness of sound in words and phrases or a pleasing pronunciation. As a technical term it describes the tendency towards greater ease in pronunciation shown in phonetic changes.

Some examples of tonality set out as contrasts include,
Clear / dull
Light / sombre
Sweet / harsh
Smooth / rough

The tonality of speech is related to the organs of speech and the habits acquired socially. From the point of view of socio-linguistics the way a person speaks, diction, indicates class identity (the Pygmalion effect). Unless there is a specific speech defect or a physical anomaly such as a cleft palate, the tonality of speech can be modified intentionally. This is similar to playing a musical instrument; the way of drawing a bow across a violin string may create a pleasant or an unpleasant sound. When creating the sounds of speech it is possible to modulate the voice to produce a range of tones. During childhood such voice modulation is a natural reaction to your close family and social circle but during the teenage years an element of conscious modulation may occur; this becomes an expression of your personality.

The circumstances of speaking will also have an influence on the tonality of speech. Cicely Berry has pointed out that urban life, especially in large cities, tends to create faster and sharper speech. Living in rural areas tends to create slower and more musical speech (1). This will be explored later when we consider the impact of 'attitude' on speech.

Pitch.

The pitch of the speaking voice may be high or low. Everyone has a natural pitch level which is largely influenced by the anatomy of the body and the vocal organs. The male voice is generally lower in pitch than for females; this change occurs at puberty and is recognised as the time when 'the voice breaks'. Young boys usually have clear treble singing voices which are more resonant than a girl's voice of equivalent age.

Pitch level can be influenced by circumstances – in a moment of fear the voice may rise noticeably in pitch. This can happen in a performance when tension in the actor results in a higher pitch and the words are pushed at the audience. Control of the pitch level is an important element in characterisation. A rising pitch is used to indicate a question or doubt and a descending pitch tends to indicate a statement or decision.

Volume.

The volume level of the voice is described as loud or soft (quiet). Speaking loudly with a high volume of sound tends to indicate confidence, approval or great joy. A lower volume level is used in intimate speech and relates to the proximity of the speaker to the listeners. Increasing or decreasing the volume of speech may indicate corresponding feelings about confidence or relationship. Volume in speaking may be linked to emotion and feeling; a raised level can express excitement while a low level or soft voice may express sadness, doubt, uncertainty or fear.

In a performance the volume of the voice also needs to relate to the acoustics of the playing space. This may be significant in a large theatre but is usually not a serious factor in chamber theatre. However, care should be taken that increasing the volume of speech does not raise the pitch. Before a performance it is wise to check out the room to feel how your voice carries; heavy curtains are sound absorbing and you may need to adjust your speaking accordingly.

Speaking at high volume is a device to be used to create a specific effect and is usually of short duration. Prolonged shouting is likely to be counter-productive in chamber theatre where the audience is so close to the players.

Pace.

Pace, or tempo, describes the rate of speaking. Pace of speaking may be linked to power of delivery. Generally a slow rate of speaking may indicate a measure of deliberation whilst a fast pace (often with increased volume) may indicate an increase in the intensity of feeling such as excitement or anger. Increasing the pace of speaking may be used to indicate a point of climax, and slowing down is a commonly used way to indicate an ending or closure.

The speed of speaking is closely related to an audience being able to hear and understand the words. Remember 'Murphy's Law' – "Always speak more slowly than you speak". Generally you should speak more slowly in performance than you think necessary; you do need to be constantly aware that the audience is hearing your words for the first time. Allow time for your voice to travel across the room, be heard and to be understood.

Don't gabble or swallow your words, enunciate clearly; always be in full control of your words. As a performer you use words to create word pictures in a way that a painter uses the colours from his palette; don't paint with muddy words, keep your words clear and colourful.
It follows that you will need to control the pace of speaking in passages of excitement or anger. This is important when speech is accelerating to enhance feeling. The practice sentences given later can be used to illustrate this point.

Avoid 'droning', speaking without variation of pitch or pace. The human animal shares in common with other mammals the ability to tune out sounds once they are identified as not posing a threat. Monotonous speaking sends a signal to the brain that this is sound without information and so one can tune out safely. Keep your performance interesting and lively, using variations in pace, volume and the pitch of your voice.

Attitude.

The elements mentioned above, tone, pitch, volume and pace, are the basic and 'physical' voice indicators. They are used in combination with a wide range of 'interpretive' voice indicators. The following short, and very selective, list indicates the range and variations of associated positive and contrasting situational attitudes; you can add to these examples from your own experience and you should use them in your practice work.

Affirmation / negation   (certainty, positive / denial)
Amusement / displeasure   (pleasing, funny / disagreeable, offensive)
Anger / calm   (cross, rage, fury / composure, restrained)

Argumentative / agreement (disputing / acceptance)
Concern / unconcerned   (interested, attentive / disinterest, indifference)
Familiar / polite   (family, friend, social / acquaintance, stranger)
Fear / trust   (apprehension / confidence)
Formal / informal   (correct, precise, conventional / relaxed, natural)
Happiness / sadness   (well-being, laughing, smiling / sorrow, unhappy)
Hope / despair   (expectation, possibility / hopeless, depression)
Like / dislike   (pleasant / unpleasant, detest, repugnance)
Love / hate.   (affinity, like, adoration / aversion, dislike)
Negative / positive   (disbelief, doubt, contradiction, cynicism /
                        certainty, confidence, decisive, assertive)
Personal / impersonal (intimate, familiar/ unconcerned, formal)
Persuade / demand   (cajole, suggest, flatter / impose, command)
Questioning / Knowing (curious, enquiring, amazement / certain, sure)
Sorrow / Joy   (sadness, regret / happiness, pleasure)
Superior / inferior   (better, dominant / insignificant, subordinate)
Suspicion / trust   (doubt, mistrust / belief, confidence)

When practising words and sentences, be aware of the impact of such different attitudes. There may be variations of degree and variations of contrasting attitudes. A dialogue line that conveys a feeling of pleasure may range from simple happiness through an expression of amusement to being comical or outrageously funny. The same line can be expressed with contrasting feelings; these may range from being mildly unpleasant to disagreeable to becoming openly offensive. Each different attitude can be interpreted by word inflection and may be accompanied by a related facial expression and gesture. All these will be explored in due course.

Voice inflection.
In performance the interpretation of a text is influenced by a range of inflections in the voice. The following examples demonstrate how some of the influences may be used. Work through these and then add in more variations of your own (you can use the above list of selected 'attitude factors' to trigger the gamut of variations). All sentences should be spoken aloud in performance mode; if you do not have a co-operative partner or younger sibling for your audience try out this practice work on the dog (alive or stuffed – you will find a patient audience who will be both appreciative and understanding). However, to explore the widest range of situations it is advisable to work with a partner – the sex and age of your partner will have an influence on your voice inflections.

    "The cup is on the table".

Start by giving equal value to each word.
Then answer the following questions by placing the stress on the relevant word in the answer to the question.

> What is on the table?
> What is the cup on?
> Is the cup under the table?
> The cup is not on the table, is it?

Interpretation by inflection.
In the above sentence the meaning was made clear by the stress on a single word. Now we can begin to interpret meaning using a combination of word inflection together with situational attitude indicators.

Starting with a single word, imagine different situations and circumstances in which the word can be used, e.g. use the word as,
> An answer to a simple question.
> A strong assertion.
> An expression of doubt.
> A question.

Try speaking without any facial expression, then repeat with what you feel as an appropriate facial expression and/or a hand movement for each occasion. You may find it helpful to say aloud what each situation is and then answer it,

a) The answer to a simple direct question, 'Do you know?', 'Will you do this?'
b) The answer to a pleasant or an unpleasant question.
c) The answer to a serious/flippant/controversial question.
d) A direct proposal/command which is welcome/unwelcome.
e) You are uncertain about your answer.
f) You are emphatic about your answer – positive/negative.
g) You are standing in front of and looking directly at the questioner.
h) You are standing with your back to the questioner.
i) You are walking towards/away from the questioner/going upstairs/downstairs.
j) You know the questioner well/intimately/a stranger/potential adversary.
k) The question is posed as friendly/objective enquiry/hostile.
l) The questioner is your equal/superior/inferior/a child.
m) Express your answer as another question/rhetorical question.

Making your own written list of possible answers may be helpful and to start with you might aim to list at least twenty different situations using different voice inflections.

> "Yes"
> "No"
> "Yes I will"   –   "No I won't"
> "Yes I can"   –   "No I can't"
> "Yes I do"   –   "Yes I did"
>
> "No I don't"   –   "No I didn't"
> "No I don't think I can do that"
> "We must do what we can"
> "What did you say"?
>
> "Can you do it"?
> "Really"
> "Of course"
> "I know"
> "I know that"
>
> "Do you want to go"?
> "Do you really think s/he meant it"?
> "Will you jump off the moon with me"?

This is a word game with a purpose; you are exploring the whole gamut of human experience and inter-action. Even a single word can be inflected to express different meanings and these, in turn, can be modified by volume, pitch or pace of speaking. The physical relationship and the distance apart of the speakers will also affect the meaning of the words – side by side, facing towards or away from each other, moving or static, standing, sitting or lying down.

As you will realize, the range of possible interpretations is almost unlimited. The intention of the exercise is to make you aware of the power of words in relation to human experiences. You should carry this understanding with you as you work on a text for performance.

Interpretation devices.
From the fore-going practice work you can see how the meaning of a sentence can be modified by introducing variations in your voice by tone, pitch, volume and pace of speaking.

Other influences on the interpretation of words will involve facial expressions, gestures and indicators of attitude. Mostly these will be intuitive movements and understood generally. The 'attitude indicators' listed earlier can be used as you vary the inflection of your words. Work with a partner, preferably of the opposite sex, as this will introduce an added depth of meaning to your words.

Explore the possible meaning of each sentence by expressing them as being said with varying attitudes such as amusement, in anger, with fear, or as a feeling of love, disdain or hate. As you add to your repertoire of interpretation devices you will intuitively discover appropriate gestures to accompany the words; these will vary in different and specific situations and will also be specific to any particular character you are portraying.

Repeat the basic sentences using an associated facial expression (e.g. raised eyebrows or a frown) and then add in hand and arm gestures. We will consider these in detail later as we explore the potential of non-verbal communication, but initially you should use the intuitive movements that occur to you naturally; these are likely to be the ones that are universally understood.

Placing the stressed word.
Where you place the stress in a sentence can affect its meaning. Try out the following sentences placing the emphasis on each word in turn. Start by stressing a single word in each sentence and then when you have done so with each word in turn, choose two words to stress in each sentence.

"I know you like red shoes".

"I like your poem / shoes / hairstyle".

"I know what you mean when you say red".

Where you place the emphasis can result in a precise intention in meaning. When you have 'rung the changes' with the word stress, speak the sentence giving equal stress value to every word. In this case notice how the intention (interpretation) of the sentence changes into a non-committal statement.

Try saying each sentence as a statement and then as a question.

Vary your attitude – confidential, argumentative or provocative.

The emphasis in a sentence can be increased by vowel elongation in a selected word; as you say these stressed words draw out the vowel. Notice how you may feel the need to vary the pitch and/or the volume in saying these words.

> "You must *try* to remember".
> "This is truly a *great* opportunity".
> "*What* did you *say*"?

Creating a climax.

Tension can be created by a series of ascending steps ending with a climax; this can be achieved by an ascending scale in pitch, increase in volume or an accelerated rate of delivery, and often a combination of these.

Try out some of these variations in the following sentences. Then try speaking them with a deliberate and even stress on what you think are the key words.

> "I'm fed up with your great sorrow, your tea-leaves and your bleeding hearts"! (2)

> "There will be no disobedience while I'm in charge".

> "You can drown me, shoot me or hang me by the neck"!

> "Is what you say really true"?

> "Do you really believe what you are saying"?

A falling inflection tends to suggest finality or certainty, or it may be used to express scorn or rudeness.

A rising inflection suggests friendliness or a question – this opens the way for the listener to respond or participate further. In most cases, after building to a climax there will follow a natural pause; this allows the hearers to appreciate the full impact of the words.

Listen and learn.

You will learn much by listening to other people speaking. Listen carefully without looking at them (this is not an open suggestion to eaves-drop). Listen how the volume and texture of the voice changes and the variety in pitch and tone occurring in everyday conversation; note the changes in speed and rhythm of speech. Notice particularly how many sentences are left unfinished in normal conversation.

The author of a crafted story will tend to write complete sentences unless the intention is to simulate normal conversation precisely. You need to be aware of this in the performance of dialogue and use the manner of speaking appropriate to the characters and their situations.

In performance with other players listen with the same concentration as you would in normal conversation and hear what is said with understanding. Sometimes in a play, with less experienced actors this listening to other speakers is replaced by just waiting to speak and listening for the next cue. Be aware constantly of what is being said and the story as it unfolds; at all times *be involved*.

The Pause and silence.

Not speaking is an important element in text interpretation. There is a well-used saying that 'silence speaks louder than words'. In a performance, silence may be accompanied by some non-verbal communication – this is the essence of mime where a single gesture or movement can convey the equivalent of a whole sentence of words.

A pause is a short silence in a sentence; it is an integral part of the performance of a text. A pause should relate to the ear and not to the eye. The pause is a moment in the text that is intuitively felt; it has no special punctuation indicator apart from the regular full stop (period point) which marks a pause between sentences. However, when marking a script for performance a slash indicator may be inserted to indicate a pause (see below).

Try saying the following sentences using a 'pregnant pause' suggested by the repeated period points; this is an exploitation of silence. You are likely to find yourself intuitively using an associated facial expression or hand gesture.

"Do you . . . "?

"You know . . . "

"Do you know . . . "?

"You are sure . . . "?

When spoken as questions the words would normally have a rising inflection with perhaps a long stress on the words 'know' and 'sure'. A different interpretation can be created if the voice is lowered on the final word.

An accompanying facial expression or gesture can create a complete sentence in the pause (innuendo). A single hand gesture can confirm a statement or leave a question open – use one finger or both hands, palms facing outwards or down, and explore different meanings as part of the pause.

Facial expressions can be added to modify the words spoken or the unspoken pause. "*Do you . . . ?*", followed by raised eyebrows can be interpreted differently if followed by a brief toss of the head as dismissal.

In performance the pause is important,
1. It allows your listeners a moment to take in what you have just said, and
2. It allows you to digest any feed-back from the audience.
3. It draws attention and adds weight to the last word(s) spoken.
4. It draws attention to a following spoken or unspoken word or thought.

A function of the pause is to ensure that words are properly audible and intelligible in addition to increasing their emotional impact and meaning. The pause is an important element in performance; but beware, if it is over-done it becomes boring.

Several types of pause can be identified.
Grammatical pause; these are indicated by the punctuation of text much as you read a musical score with its notes and rests.

The time value of a musical note is written as a semibreve, minim, crotchet or quaver. These notes and the rests in between notes (periods of silence) are given specific symbols indicating the time to be allowed. Punctuation of a text may be interpreted in a similar way. The time value of a full stop (period point) or colon is twice as long as the time value of a comma or semi-colon. Proponents of Readers Theatre often give the general guidance of counting to measure these; for a comma or semi-colon, count 1, for a full stop, or period point, count 1, 2. The pause between the end of a paragraph and the beginning of the next, can be counted as 1, 2, 3.

A practical way to indicate the relative time value of a pause, as mentioned above, is to use a slash mark at the appropriate place in the text. One slash for a brief pause, two slashes for a longer pause. When marking a script these pause marks may be written in coloured pencil to draw attention to them. The actual time value in text punctuation is not regulated by a metronome as in music, but is an intuitive moment varying with each particular text and situation (including the audience response) and comes with practice and experience in reading aloud.

Sense pause; this is an intuitive pause to enhance meaning in a sentence.

Emphatic pause; this may be used before or after an important word or phrase. A prefatory pause holds the listener's attention and prepares for the impact of the following words. A following pause allows time for the significance of the previous word(s) to be appreciated.

Emotional pause; this is used as an interpretation of feeling. The specific emotion may be spoken as a reporting clause, but most frequently it is expressed in the manner of performance, e.g. anger, despair or extreme sadness, with an appropriate accompanying facial expression, gesture or action.

Dramatic pause; it may be argued that this is a cover-all term for all types of pause. The intention of a dramatic pause is to hold the attention of the listeners in order for the effect of the words to register or to prepare the audience for the following words. (A very strong dramatic pause may be marked in your script by three slashes.)

With practice you will acquire an intuitive sensing when to pause; the rhythm of the words is your guide. You will also discover that the pause gives increased power to the words; pausing can give emphasis and brings attention to a particular word or phrase. This 'power of the pause' also allows you to introduce facial expressions and gestures to enhance interpretation and to indicate the author's movement of thought. A mimed action can be introduced within the pause to convey the unspoken words. Rodenburg expresses this succinctly, "When you speak you seed the thought or image; in the pause it grows to full flower".

The silence may be interpreted variously by individuals in the audience but usually follows a general consensus of understanding – raising the eye-brows, angle of the head, shrugging shoulders, a wink, up-turned palms – these are all gestures which can convey a complete sentence without speech. But their interpretation will relate to the nature of the character and the situation. The speed at which the gesture is made will also be relevant and influence its interpretation. All the practice sentences given above can be used to vary the interpretation, e.g. try speaking the sentence '*I know you like red shoes*' with different facial expressions, head and hand gestures.

In a performance of 'Theatre of the Imagination' a mimed sequence may accompany a passage of spoken text or it may follow a speech to add emphasis or illustration. At all times the actor must be plainly in sight of the audience. A seated player may need to stand in order to convey some explicit movement. Keep these thoughts in mind as you practise and you will appreciate the advice always to work with an audience, however small and seemingly insignificant; the presence of your 'audience' will help you to an awareness of communicating through the pause and unspoken gesture.

Notes.
1. Cicely Berry, *Voice and the actor*, (New York, NY, Wiley, 1973), p.8.
2. Philip King and Falkland Carey, *Sailor beware!* (London, Samuel French), 1952.

6. Non-verbal Communication.

A performance with words alone is the particular province of radio. For all other occasions, where the performer and the audience can see each other, facial expressions, gestures and body movements are integral to human communication.

The basic senses.
Non-verbal communication is involved with the senses; the five basic senses have long been recognized and named; these are, seeing, hearing, tasting, touching and smelling. Each of these senses has gradations of intensity which may be expressed by a performer through facial expressions and gestures. A further twenty senses have been suggested to add to this short list but the five basic senses are the ones fundamental to the actor. When performing a story the actor/presenter will need to convey these sensations through actions to supplement words used in the text.

The sense of *seeing* can be expressed as looking and observing. The difference can be significant, especially to an actor preparing for a role, and may be measured in degrees of intensity and timing; a trained observer may 'see' more in a brief glance than a casual onlooker might see in a longer time span. For example, an experienced visual artist will be quickly aware of line detail, shape, colour and tone that may be missed by a less skilled viewer. In performance a difference in intensity may be communicated through time value – a brief glancing movement to indicate looking, or a longer period of deliberate observation.

Seeing can also be interpreted in terms of direction. Looking directly at a person conveys a different sensation of seeing than by a sideways, upwards or downwards look. Direct looking can indicate an openness of intention, whilst a sideways glance may convey uncertainty. A downward look may involve disdain or superiority while the upward look may accompany a questioning attitude.

Similarly the general sense of *hearing* may vary in intensity ranging from an awareness of sound to a concentrated act of listening. Most listeners can distinguish between harsh and sweet sounds but subtle differences in tone and pitch may not be so obvious. A musician may be able to recognize when a passage is played in a major or minor key but for a general listener this is often a sense of feeling rather than musical knowledge. In performance, the effect of a harsh or unpleasant sound may be expressed by a 'screwed-up' tense facial expression and a pleasant sound may be accompanied by closed eyes with a relaxed facial expression. Hand gestures may be appropriate; hands in a 'welcoming' gesture may indicate a pleasing sound when used with closed or partly closed eyes. But hands over the ears can suggest a harsh or unpleasant sound.

Feeling, as a physical sense, includes touching the surface of an object or identifying a deeper sensation through pressure of softness or hardness, or as a state of heat or cold, or of wet or dry. Again, there is the matter of degree of feeling; the softness of a feather against your skin or the pressure of a hearty handclasp of a giant rugby player. Physical feeling ranges from mere sensation, through pleasant touch to the pain caused by pressure, heat or cold. In performance, appropriate hand gestures may be accompanied by a related facial expression to indicate pain or a lesser sensation, or a like or dislike reaction. The speed and degree of re-active movement may also indicate the nature of the feeling; a lingering hand or finger movement may suggest softness whereas a quick withdrawal suggests a degree of heat or pain.

The sense of *smell* may range from a general awareness of odour, such as lilacs in bloom or fried onions, to a triggered emotion aroused from a cosmetic fragrance. This sense, perhaps more than others, is conditioned by experience; to a countryman the smell of pig manure is likely to cause different reactions than it would to a town dweller. In performance, the most obvious indicator of smell would be a touching or squeezing the nose accompanied by the appropriate facial expression; closed eyes and a smile tend to suggest approval of a pleasant smell.

Tasting is a specific sense of bitter, sweet or sour. This basic sense is part of our natural survival mechanism; we are likely to spit out bitter-tasting objects but will retain sweet and savoury foods. Taste is also modified by experience; most people reject a very hot chilli pepper which an *aficionado* will relish without discomfort. In performance an appropriate facial expression involving the mouth may be augmented with a reactive gesture.

All these senses may be expressed generally in terms of like or dislike, pleasant or unpleasant. In performance mode it may not be possible to communicate a sensation specifically without words, e.g. fried onions, but it is possible to indicate a general sensation using conventional gestures. The position and movements of the head together with facial expressions can convey gradations of seeing, hearing or smelling. Closing the eyes with a smile on the lips can express a pleasant sound or smell and holding the first finger to thumb in a letter 'o' is a well-recognised expression of approval of taste. The sense of a hot object can be communicated by a sudden withdrawal movement of the hand or body accompanied with a facial expression; the degree of heat may be indicated by the speed of the movement. In performance the actor will draw on personal experience to imagine the source of the event or situation and to react accordingly.

When preparing a text for performance examine the words that express the senses; you will frequently find an intuitive gesture or a facial expression to accompany them and which illustrates the sensation. But always think around such movements to see if you can discover something less obvious but which might be more expressive.

Face and head.

Stanislavsky taught his student actors that "the eyes are the window of the soul"; so many of our inner feelings are expressed through our eyes. Cicely Berry has pointed out that "if the eyes are not communicating the voice will not be communicating completely, either" (1). In chamber theatre performances an intimate communication can be established with the audience by regular eye contact. Lines may be spoken directly at one individual using eye contact, then, by moving eye contact to others in the audience the intimate contact throughout the audience can be continued.

Even with a small audience direct eye contact has its limitations; your listeners are likely to be arranged around you with different sight-lines. Some additional physical movement may be needed. The position of the player's head is important by drawing attention to the eye direction. The head position is also used to indicate attitude; moving the head from side-to-side is conventionally interpreted as negation and up-and-down head movements indicate agreement. Build on these simple indicators to express different meanings, first with a single movement (e.g. a nod) and then with several repetitive movements, varying the speed of movement, slow and then faster; the degree of movement can be varied to further modify the meaning. Explore these head movements as the silent answer to a question (see the examples given earlier) and then accompanied with the appropriate words, "Yes", "No" and with different facial expressions.

A single nod may convey emphatic agreement and a sideways movement with a turn-away may convey emphatic disagreement or disgust. The duration, speed and intensity of the movement will also modify the meaning and interpretation. Work through as many variations as you can think of and preferably prompted by a partner; use silent movements at first and then add in words. These will not be isolated actions, you will find that your shoulders and arms will become involved in expressing the feeling. A wide range of expression is possible – a shrug of the shoulders together with both hands upturned will be interpreted differently if the hand movements are used without the shoulder shrug.

Similarly, the eyebrows can indicate attitude and feeling; this factor has greater potential in chamber theatre than in conventional stage acting. Raised eyebrows with eyes opened wide accompany surprise or disbelief, but in performance, and without a close-up camera shot, these feelings will necessarily need to incorporate associated head and body movements. The question *"Are you sure?"* may be expressed without words by movement of the eyebrows; this may be accompanied by a head movement. Raised eyebrows keep the question open whereas a frown can indicate doubt. Moving the head towards or away from the listener can introduce further depths of interpretation. Explore the '*what-do-you-think?*' silent questioning to the audience using eyes and a side-ways motion of the head; try this with a single look at one member of the audience and then taking in several persons. This illustrates the opportunities of 'sharing the text' with the audience and occurs specifically and frequently when presenting Chaucer's '*Canterbury Tales*' as the 'Chaucer Experience'; often the behaviour of the characters in the stories relate closely with modern day behaviour. (When exploring such passages, imagine yourself as Chaucer sitting amongst his friends and sharing his thoughts and experiences with them.)

Shoulders and body.
The use of full body movement is more limited in chamber theatre than in conventional stage acting. The stage area is smaller and all the players acting closely with each other are all on stage continuously throughout the performance. However, the greater proximity of the players to the audience will lead to a more direct form of communication between performers and the audience and even small movements can have meaning. Earlier performances of Readers Theatre limited walking movement with the readers standing or sitting, and speaking 'above the heads of the audience'. Over the years this has evolved into a more relaxed and dynamic approach to performance. In a chamber theatre presentation there is complete freedom of movement and players move around the acting space as required by the interpretation of the story, limited only by the acting space available.

This does not, however, involve rapid running across the stage or frequent entrances or exits. Action movement is focussed on a small playing area close to the audience. The broad 'projected' movements used in a large theatre are not needed; in the small space and actions become more 'conversational' and intimate in nature. The focus is on the shared story-telling by the players with the individuals in the audience and this approach is derived from familiar 'bed-time story-telling'. The scripts held in the hand are obvious and there is no attempt to disguise the fact that the story has not been completely memorized. The players do not 'become' the characters as in a conventional play but share each character with the listeners in specific 'cameo' presentations. You might like to think of these as illustrations or pictures within the story text in a book

The players sit at the level of the audience and 'acting' movements tend to be primarily focussed on the head, shoulders and upper body. Standing and walking are incorporated into the action of the story as required. The acts of standing up, sitting down or walking away assume a specific significance within the story and how these movements are done needs to be well thought out, practised and accomplished.

Stools or chairs can be used to enhance a range of effective body movements. After a speech delivered standing, the act of sitting will indicate a change of meaning or pace in the story. The manner and timing of sitting down and the seated posture adopted can be used to express attitude and feelings. The converse will be true of a seated player slowly or suddenly standing up – this might be followed by a spoken word or remark, or an expressive silence. The closeness of the audience can make such action intense and meaningful.

The movement of the body can be expressive in many ways. Turning or moving towards, or away from another player can be an indicator of attitude. The time value of the turn and the volume of the turn (arms held close to the body or stretched out) can indicate quite different intentions. Seen in the close-up situation of the restricted playing space such movements can have a stronger impact than might be experienced on a distant conventional theatre stage.

Kneeling can also communicate intention and feeling. A full kneel, on both knees, may indicate complete submission to the other player – who may be unseen in the context of a god. Dropping on to one knee is another deliberate act and may be accompanied by a bowing of the head; this is an acknowledgement of an unspoken difference between the two players. If the performance requires kneeling this must be carefully explored and practised to achieve fluency and clarity of meaning. Kneeling in a crouched position may convey quite different meanings and can range in interpretation from utter servility or fear to a humorous gesture of fun.

From the fore-going comments it can be appreciated that the limited space available in a chamber theatre performance can be used to great advantage. The proximity of the audience enables quite small movements to be seen and understood. Two players may convey a range of intentions and emotions; standing close to each other, face to face, may express friendship or dislike (relaxed or tense). Posture, gesture and facial expression together will convey the appropriate intention. One player moving behind another may indicate concern or involvement with an associated turn of the head, or a disconnection may be indicated if the shoulders are turned away. Working with a partner, refer back to the list of 'Attitudes' given in the previous chapter and illustrate these with appropriate movements.

Grouping arrangements of the players will be discussed later; relationships between characters can be powerfully indicated by spatial position and in themselves can indicate intentions, feelings and attitude. The presence of a third player greatly increases the possibilities of non-verbal movement.

Gesture.
There are numerous 'conventional' gestures that are universal in conveying meaning. The 'stop' sign of a raised hand outstretched with outward facing palm is well understood and used. However, when the hand is held close to the side of the body a different intention is indicated (the intention is augmented when both hands are used); the angle of the palm will also modify the interpretation.

A beckoning hand movement is similarly recognised as the *'come here'* signal. Try out a modification of this gesture using a single finger and vary it by using a steady direct eye contact and then while looking away from the beckoned person. Quite different attitudes can be expressed in such a simple movement. A full arm and hand gesture may suggest a command as seen in a traffic control situation but a single finger movement in a steady hand can be suggestive of an intention which may be elaborated through the face and eyes – a "*come hither*" situation. Explore the range of meanings by varying the degree or volume of the movement and its time value

The example sentences given earlier can be combined with the attitude indicators listed and can now be repeated using appropriate hand, arm and head gestures. Although initially you may think of these in simple ways, e.g. '*No*' with a single hand 'stop' gesture, you will soon realize that these movements can become complex as feelings are explored conveying various combinations of attitude and emotion.

'*No*' may be accompanied by a low held, sideways hand movement to indicate dismissal or 'of no consequence'; this will be interpreted differently with the hand held palm uppermost or with the palm held downwards. Then, with the palm held steadily uppermost, a rising inflection and raised shoulders and eyebrows can transform the single word into a full question; using one or both hands will modify the meaning of the gesture which can be further modified by using a single finger. Further degrees of meaning can be introduced by moving the hand, or hands, away from the body or holding them closely in; the meaning changes with the speed and the amount of movement used. One arm across the body with the elbow towards your partner and the single word '*No*' can express fear or apprehension.

Experiment with the simple words such as '*come*', '*go*', '*wait*', '*of course*', '*really*', and then move on to phrases – '*you think so*', '*I do not believe . . .*', '*if that is what you think . . .*'. Work through the list of attitude indicators (and add more from your own experience), combining speech with gesture and treating each word or sentence firstly as a statement and then repeated as a question. Explore the range of meanings with variations in voice pitch, tone, pace and volume; then experiment with placing a pause, before the word or sentence, at the end, or between words.

All these variations in hand and arm gestures will be accompanied by a facial expression or head movement which can modify the interpretation. Some of these movements might be lost when acting on a conventional theatre stage, but they can have power in the intimacy of chamber theatre.

This is not a one-off exercise. There are so many variations and possibilities that you will want to explore the whole gamut of communication, by word, facial expression, gesture and body movement. Include the actions of sitting and standing as you speak, turning in different directions, kneeling and then climbing on to a stool (which may represent a tree, a platform, a staircase or a hill). Within a text the appropriate gestures or movements may seem obvious and intuitive, but by exploring alternatives you may find new meanings behind the words and in the manner they are spoken in different situations.

Spatial relationships.

There is yet another factor to be considered relating to non-verbal communication. This is the significance of the space relationships of actor and audience, the distance and placing or position between speakers and listeners. As mentioned earlier, the intimacy of chamber theatre enables facial expressions and quite small hand gestures to have meaningful impact which might be lost on a conventional stage in a large auditorium. An expressive head movement can also be seen and understood in the small chamber audience. Such small movements are enhanced by the spatial relationships of the players.

The size and nature of an auditorium influences the presentation and the manner of speaking by the performers. In a large meeting space without sound amplification, speech becomes louder; the volume is increased in order to reach those members of the audience furthest away from the speaker. Sentences may be shortened and the delivery tends to become declamatory as an aid to understanding. In a religious context there is a tendency to ritualistic speaking or reading – deliberate delivery to convey authority in the message.

In a large auditorium with many people present the speaker needs to be raised up in order to be seen. A speaker who cannot be seen clearly will have difficulty in being heard (a factor well understood in theatrical stage lighting). Rodenburg makes this point clear, "There is a direct link between seeing a face and hearing a voice" (2).The raised voice of the speaker is accompanied by gestures that need to be somewhat larger than would be used with smaller groups. Each movement of the hand or head must be seen clearly and be interpreted by the audience 'in the back row'. The 'close-up' of film is not possible on the conventional stage, thus small facial movements will need to be augmented by larger associated movements of the head and shoulders. The predominant effect is that of 'telling', or getting one's message across in a one-directional flow of words.

In a smaller auditorium, such as a classroom, the speaker's voice can be lowered in volume as the listeners are closer. Here there is inter-activity between speaker and listeners and the general atmosphere is that of 'sharing' and the tone of voice can be modified accordingly. The closer relationship may be further indicated by the speaker (teacher) moving out from behind a lectern or desk and often with some walking amongst the listeners.

The general atmosphere is further relaxed in the tutorial room where there are even fewer listeners. Everyone sits at the same level and voices are kept at normal conversational level. 'Sharing' is an essential element in the tutorial interchange between the participants. This can be similar to the relationships present in the chamber theatre performance.

Normal social distance between individuals in most Western cultures is around four to five feet; this may be generally accepted as a 'comfort zone'. This distance may change as the group becomes more formal or more informal. A formal meeting between two or three persons may be determined by the dominant speaker who may sit or stand behind a desk. If no furniture is present the formal or dominant relationship may be indicated by holding some object, e.g. a book, or even a piece of paper, as a separation device.

A gathering of three or four persons as friends or family, brings closer proximity and a familiar relationship with a corresponding ease of speaking. This is a close social group where the distance between each other is around three feet. At this distance the relationship is familiar and generally confident between everyone present; there is frequent eye contact and touching and the speech is correspondingly lowered to conversational levels. If anger or conflict enters this situation there may be some drawing apart together with added muscle tension and raised voices.

Finally, the very close relationship of two intimates with a distance of less than two feet brings soft and quiet speaking, often whispering in close proximity with frequent touching. This intimate distance relationship will be further modified when standing, sitting or lying down beside each other. All these may be considered as normal personal distances and variations will indicate special circumstances, e.g. as indicated above, where a teenager and parent in argument one or other will increase the inter-personal distance and the voice volume may also be increased. Interpretation will be further modified by the speakers moving forwards or away from each other, suggesting agreement or disagreement and by the variation in position of the body, head or shoulders.

Practice into performance.
The practice sentences that you have been using may now be repeated placing them in the context of specific relationship distances. A spoken '*No*' will have a different volume, tone and meaning before a large political meeting, or to a congregation in church, or a teacher in a classroom or tutorial room, or when whispered between two lovers on a

couch (this may be further modified when words are spoken lying in bed together).

In order to become an accomplished performer you will need to practise. A musician will spend several hours a day practising; the more expert one becomes the more one practises. This applies equally to the speech performer. Your chosen instruments are your voice and body. You will need to explore how to use these to produce sounds and a performance that an audience will want to hear, and one that they can relate to and understand.

Practise with words and sounds to communicate different meanings. Also practise the variations of facial expressions and hand gestures to communicate meaning. Combine voice (words) and movement (face and gesture) to explore the fullest possible interpretation of the text. This is similar to the way that a musician might practice a composition, seeking to feel the intentions of the composer and the player's own inner feelings.

Working with a partner is always recommended. Notice how the meaning of words can change when spoken in different situations and by the different physical positions and attitudes (of both partners). Words and gestures may be interpreted differently when in same-sex or opposite-sex situations. Meaning will also be influenced by movement – as you approach or move away. A spoken '*No*' when walking away will convey a different intention than when the word is spoken when standing face-to-face and different again if the speaker takes a step forwards. A further variation with your practice sentences might be added by a visualized situation where you are both on different levels such as on a stairway, and going up towards the other person or going down away from him or her. Explore this situation with variations in the tone and volume of voice and then include differences in age or sex. A range of subtle meanings and intentions can be introduced.

All the simple practice sentences given earlier can be varied with different combinations of voice inflections, attitudes, gestures and movements. Try speaking in a direct face-to-face position (imagined or with a partner), then with your back turned, and then again with the words spoken 'over your shoulder'. These positions can be varied; both sitting or both standing, or one sitting and the other standing. In the latter case the way the words are interpreted will change as the speaker stands or sits. These variations in Pace, Volume or Tone should be explored with different levels of each and with an increase or decrease in each indicator. Work through as many variations as you can think of with your partner.

How many different meanings can be put on each word that you stress –
by voice, facial expression or gesture? This may seem to be an amusing
game with each partner trying to find new meanings in words and gestures
but what you are exploring here is the whole gamut of human inter-
relationships and communication of feelings and intentions.

When you think that you may have exhausted all possibilities with all
variations and combinations, try them again, but this time inserting a
Pause in between words. Work through each sentence with the pause in
different places. Think these pauses through with different attitudes – your
attitude may change after the pause – then interpret the pause using an
appropriate gesture or facial expression.

Human speech is as varied as the sounds of music. In speech we use the
instrument of our own voice and body, it is voice music. Speech can be
powerful and expressive of our feelings and intentions whether we are
speaking to one person or to many. Through performance we breathe life
into written words and in chamber theatre we share those words and
experiences with our audience in an especially intimate way. The actress
Jill Balcon described performance as beyond technique, "phrasing, lyric
impulse, submission of self, these have to be drawn out of someone in
whom they do exist" (3)

Interpretation – voice and body.
Performing a crafted text is an act of interpretation. All voice inflections,
including the all-powerful pause and silence, and all gestures, must be
rooted in the text. Together they tell the story in a particular way, a story
shared always with the audience. In chamber theatre the audience is
brought into the story by the attitude of the performer, by voice and by the
unspoken gestures.

The practice work outlined above can be considered to be only an
introduction to the exploration of human inter-actions; the variations you
work with will come from your own and your partner's personal
experiences and will inevitably be limited. Expand this experience by
observing human behaviour around you. Become aware of how people
behave in different circumstances, in the office or your workplace, in
shops or in the street, observe their mannerisms, gestures and way of
speaking. As you 'collect people' in this way you may find yourself
taking note of how people behave on television – in the news items and in
documentaries. The actors in many films are highly competent in
portraying 'real-life' behaviour and observing them in a range of
situations can increase your repertoire of interpretations. Look for the

'close-ups' and for the small gestures and movements. Some of these are part of the mannerisms of certain well-known actors. A line, phrase, intonation or gesture may be repeated by an actor in quite different stories and situations.

In chamber theatre performance feedback from the audience can be more palpable and more direct than when acting in a large auditorium. The audience response time is shorter. However, this is not an argument to 'play to the audience', rather that the players can feel reactions which reinforce the intended thrust of the performance. The more frequently that you perform in these small spaces and intimate surroundings the more easily you will be aware of this feed-back.

Use the practice sentences to try out the variations in interpretation; They are exercises in voice 'music'. This is the voice equivalent of practising the scales, ornaments and phrasing devices used in music, e.g. arpeggio, mordant and staccato. When you are familiar with the basic techniques you can apply them as required in a text.

From the practice sentences move on to the performance of texts; the poems and speeches of Shakespeare are particularly useful. Expand your practice by selections from poetry or prose of your own choosing. The measured prose of Charles Dickens or of Jane Austen, provide a wealth of material before tackling modern authors. Select passages of description as well as dialogue; you will find suitable material on your own bookshelves. After that you can explore the shelves of your public library, and many more texts are available online through the Internet (see Appendix C).

Notes.
1. Ciceley Berry, *Voice and the Actor*, (New York, Wiley, 1973), p.130.
2. Patsy Rodenburg, *The Actor Speaks, voice and the performer*, (London, Methuen Drama, 1997) p. 302.
3. Jill Balcon, quoted in Josephine J. Johnson, *Return of the Scops; English poetry performance since 1961,* in Thompson, ibid. p.301.

7. Performance Mode.

The general term 'performance' embraces the interpretation of a text through words and movement. Sometimes words may be omitted, as occurs in mime or dance, or visual movement may be omitted as in radio story-telling/drama. In chamber theatre both speech and movement are used to perform and interpret a crafted story text using both spoken narration and acted dialogue.

Brecht regarded 'narrative' as the soul of drama (1) and in a stage play the narrative is contained within the stage setting, the dialogue and the presentation of the actors. The performers of chamber theatre use explicit spoken narration and dialogue to stimulate the imagination of the audience to "fill in the pieces" of the story in the absence of the conventional stage 'experience'. Brecht's ideal audience was "a critical, intellectually engaged and questioning audience". One tactic he used was the ploy of leaving the house lights up in the auditorium; this was designed to encourage the audience to view social conditions in a new light. With chamber theatre this is not a ploy but a natural and integral part of the performance; everyone in the audience is necessarily involved with what they see and hear, they are not simply spectators or observers.

Entering performance mode.
After all your rehearsal and practice the moment arrives for your public appearance, and this moment itself requires preparation. In a similar way that an athlete before a race will 'limber up' to loosen muscles ready for intensive action, so the performer needs to release tension in body and mind to enable communication with the audience.

Every actor has a degree of 'fear' or apprehension before going on stage; this state of emotion releases adrenaline into the blood stream which assists a heightened state of readiness. However, this natural tension may constrict easy breathing and prevent clear voice production. There may be tension in the shoulders or the spine may be slumped or too rigid, and the jaw may be held too tightly. These tensions will affect voice production; as a way of loosening up the following preparatory routine can be used before a performance.

- Before every performance find a quiet place for your simple preparatory practice. Start with a few deep breaths with eyes closed.

- Stand in the full support position, head, spine and feet in line, toes slightly turned out.
- Be aware of the position of the spine, pelvis flat, not tilted forwards, body weight transferring through thighs and knees to heels and feet.
- Stomach and abdominal muscles relaxed, not pulled in or forced out.
- In this state of readiness,

  Rotate the head clockwise several times, then, repeat with an anti-clockwise motion.

  Turn head to the right and then to the left, extending the muscles and tendons.

  Shoulders should hang naturally; rotate right, then left shoulder several times, forwards then backwards.

  Move the lower jaw to loosen muscles, yawn and 'chew' for several seconds.

  Start to voice sounds,

  Begin with humming, start with a high pitch and move down the scale, then, repeat with the sound going up the scale.

  Voice the long vowels, A, E, O, U, following different consonants, particularly B, M, P.

  Then voice the vowels followed by R.

  Keep the head and neck in the support position and exaggerate the movement of the muscles of the face, mouth and lips.

This warm-up preparation will be somewhat different for chamber theatre than when acting in a conventional theatre. Without a separate dressing-room an appropriate space may not be available. However, this limber-up procedure is needed for the highest state of readiness to perform. With a cast of only three players the warm-up may be done as a group activity.

There is one final point before you 'go onstage'. The routine outlined above is designed to enable you to release tension in your body and to begin to concentrate on what you are going to do next; this concentration will help to allay your fears as you move in front of the audience. But this is not the relaxation you feel after a sauna. Cicely Berry prefers to use the word 'free' rather than 'relaxed'; free implies being relaxed but ready for action, alert but not tense. This is the springboard to action; the poised stance of a fencer or a dancer ready to move with the first bars of the music. It is the state of coiled readiness for action (2).

Narration.

There may be one or more narrators in performing the story and they may use direct or indirect speech. Without the conventions of a stage play, e.g. scenery, costumes or stage movements, narration in chamber theatre needs careful presentation. A natural instinct may be to have a single narrator who will speak in a normal voice which is emotionally neutral. Some players like to use a specific form of their normal voice such as the way they might answer on the telephone. This could be a neutral, professionally sounding voice that is slightly more modulated than normal. It may occasionally be appropriate for the narrator to use a 'regional' voice to set the scene.

Sometimes in 'setting the scene' you may use emotion in the narration; this may involve a vocal tremor or a change of pace in speaking to match the words. The dialogue sections will then be distinguished by using the full range of voice and attitude indicators.

Narrative passages may be spoken more slowly than you may feel you should speak. Remember that the audience is hearing the words for the first time and in the narration you are 'setting the scene' and 'indicating characters'; both are essential to understand the story. Important words or phrases may be high-lighted in your script and these may be emphasised slightly. Be aware that the cultural and knowledge background of the audience will be a factor in their understanding and interpretation of the words you are using.

Dialogue.

Actors in a conventional stage play are selected and cast according to gender, age, and physical appearance as well as their acting skills. The performance of dialogue conveys and reinforces each character by the use of appropriate voice, gesture and movement associated with the actor's costume and make-up.

The performer in chamber theatre combines dialogue with narration and moves seamlessly between them. Voice and gesture develop the characterisation but in this form of story-telling there is no specific 'casting' and a player may need to cross the boundaries of age or physical appearance. Even the distinctions of gender may be blurred. One practical approach where the text contains much dialogue is for a cast to include two male and two female players with a difference in their ages (this can be a useful approach in a performance of Benét's narrative poem '*John Brown's Body*'. Generally, if only three players are involved either an all-female group may be used, or one male and two female players may be preferred.

The open text.
There is a significant difference when performing chamber theatre from acting on a conventional stage. The stage actor memorizes the complete dialogue text for a specific character but the chamber theatre player performs with an open text and includes some memorization in particular sections of the story.

Working with an open text, a script in your hand, instead of learning all your lines and transforming yourself into a stage character, is an acquired technique; it is not 'natural' for actors to do this, they want to learn their lines and 'own' the words in order to develop their character. But it is natural to work with a text in this way for performed, and shared, literary story-telling. When you have fully accepted this as normal practice your audience will also accept your performance.

It is important that you hold and use the script as an integral part of your hand and body. For this reason a small size script is recommended; an A5 size binder may be used but a script tablet may be preferred. The latter consists of a single stiff board approximately 9"x7" with two binding rings; this enables easy holding of the script and page 'turning' with the minimum of distraction. Other scripts may be inter-changed and inserted as needed.

Performing text.
Performing a literary text as a chamber theatre performance differs from a conventional stage play in several respects. The players are normally on stage all the time and dramatic entrances and exits are rarely needed. At the beginning, the players need to enter with confidence and expectation as they take up their pre-arranged starting positions. In early presentations of Readers Theatre the readers were placed behind lecterns/music stands. In present-day chamber theatre the scripts are carried openly in view and are integral to the player and the performance; free movement is encouraged.

Hand-held scripts need to be considered in terms of the performance action. The hand-held script can be used as an extension of the player's arm (perhaps not unlike the racquet in the hand of a tennis player) and should be seen as a natural part of the performance. The script should be held at a convenient level where lines may be read by a downward glance without undue movement of the head; only the eyes should move. The natural use of the script must be clearly established from the very beginning of the performance as the players enter with the scripts held either at their side or with both hands in front. The ways of handling the script become an integral part of every rehearsal and all movements should be smooth and inconspicuous. Excessive head movement to read is distracting and suggests a lack of confidence by the player.

Some appropriate early hand movements may be made with the 'script arm' to identify the essential presence of the script but subsequent hand gestures can be made by the free hand. A player may be seen to read part of a line obviously and to complete the line by speaking directly to the audience with eye contact. This sharing of the text with the audience will establish the script as part of the performance.

The nature of the action needs to be considered. Playing a love scene or a fight scene with swords can rarely be convincing even with a script held 'naturally' in hand. Two possible alternatives are, either that two players may speak while others mime the action, or, that these, usually short episodes, may be fully memorized and acted without scripts. Such episodes should be incorporated smoothly into the performance.

It is in such stage action that the differences between chamber theatre and conventional acting are most apparent. In a conventional play the actors identify completely with their allotted character, owning the words, movements and gestures; the action is performed in 'real time' for the story. In chamber theatre the actors are performing story-tellers; they are sharing the characters and the action in 'real-time' with the audience. They narrate the story and illustrate the action in a somewhat similar way that pictures are inserted into a book text. Here they are not simulating a real-life situation; they are illustrating specific actions or events in the story by performance. (This reflects the approach of Guazzo in the seventeenth century where he considered oral performance within the context of social conversation) (3).

When acting in this 'illustration mode' the script becomes subordinate to the action and thus the script hand may merge into the background. If this cannot be achieved convincingly, then other players may illustrate the particular action without scripts.

Sitting comfortably

Unlike performing in a conventional theatre each venue for chamber theatre will be different, unfamiliar and unique. A general seating arrangement for the audience is likely to adapt the Host's normal furniture arrangement to one approaching a modified horse-shoe style; the audience seated around the players on three sides. However, seating in a private drawing-room will vary greatly often with dining chairs and bean-bags interspersed with sofas.

A performance of chamber theatre may also take place in a library room, a school classroom or in a museum or other 'heritage' building. In such circumstances the 'hosts' may have conventional 'theatre style' seating arrangements. The strict formality of blocks of chairs is best avoided, at the very least a simple horse-shoe arrangement can be used, preferably with no more than two rows of seats and these should be staggered to provide full viewing by everyone present. A maximum of 'forty-plus' seats only should be allowed; any larger group will destroy the intimacy of the occasion. Seating arrangements should be discussed with the Host to ensure safety of movement with optimum informality for viewing pleasure.

The seating arrangements for the players will vary according to the text to be performed. Unlike a stage play, the players are most likely to start a performance from a sitting position sharing the same level as the audience. On a conventional stage actors may be 'discovered' in position or they walk on from the wings. In chamber theatre the players walk into the room at the commencement and may sit down while the performance is introduced.

The initial seating arrangement need only be regarded as 'starting positions' as the nature of the performance will create fluid movements within the acting space. The players will hold their scripts in hand throughout the performance without the use of lecterns. All movements with the scripts should be natural. Familiarity with the text will usually tend towards more memorization of the words and freer movement.

Grouping arrangements.

The position of the actors, where they stand or move in relation to each other is another example of non-verbal communication. Some aspects of spatial relationships have been touched on earlier. The following notes can by illustrated and explored in practice by using the attitude indicators given earlier; use the practice sentences and combine words with movements to create different meanings and interpretations.

When standing, the grouping and movement of the players will be similar to conventional stage action except the degree of movement will be restricted by the more confined acting space. Even one person can make an attitude statement by the position taken on the stage in relation to the audience, by body posture and the movements made. A player standing very close to the individuals in the front row may be interpreted as being very friendly and intimate or it could be a tense stance of aggression. The accompanying facial expression and body pose will clarify which attitude is intended.

Two players have more opportunities of relational positioning to use in indicating attitudes. Side by side suggests a collaboration or agreement with each other. In contrast, by standing well apart and facing each other suggests a difference of opinion or opposition. The accompanying facial and body stance will clarify their intentions; hand and arm movements will also express feelings and attitudes. Both hands held down by the side will have a different interpretation than if the elbows are bent or whether the hands are open or closed in fists, with or without tension. Further variations of intention can be indicated by movement towards or away from each other or by simply turning the head or body towards or away. Use the practice sentences to explore different interpretations of grouping and movement.

With a three-player group the range of potential attitudes becomes even greater. This is the fundamental stage triangle and its simple geometric pattern can be used to illustrate different actor relationships. Specific attitudes will be indicated by the use of facial expression, gesture or movement towards or away from each other. The actor at the apex of a triangle furthest from the audience may be seen as being 'dominant' and attracting special attention (a fact that some actors have been known to use in order to 'upstage' other actors and to draw attention to themselves). There is less space in chamber theatre to exploit the acting triangle as extensively as it is used on the conventional stage, nevertheless it has significance in demonstrating relationships and intentions between the players.

Limitations in performance.
In the small acting space available walking movement will be limited and for much of the time an actor may be required to perform 'on the spot'. The degree of movement will be influenced by the nature of the story to be told, the player's interpretation of the text and the director's intentions for the performance. This is where the term 'Theatre of the Imagination'

again comes into focus and where the detail of voice inflection, face and gesture gain in importance.

Seated players may use lecterns but it is usually preferable to hold their scripts in hand. (If lecterns are used they should be adjusted for convenient reading and placed in front and slightly to one side of the player to avoid obscuring the player's face from the audience.) Seated players will be at the same level with their seated audience in telling the story and then, by standing up special attention can be drawn to the following acted (movement) section.

Players need to hold the head up in order to maintain eye contact with the audience and only glance down momentarily to read as necessary. This upright position is also necessary in order to keep the airway open and to enable smooth breathing and effective voice production. Familiarity with the text is important and the amount of rehearsal time is significant. The more the script is rehearsed the greater opportunity there will be to become familiar with the text and to memorize lines. This leads to greater freedom in acting and opens up opportunities to explore different interpretations of the text.

Particular attention should be paid to the occasions of rising and sitting which should be carefully rehearsed. Movement should always be smooth and slow or fast according to the text interpretation, but should not be made as a sudden or unexpected move. Usually some indication can be given by voice or gesture that a change is about to happen. The players may then move smoothly into the action. The return to the seated position should be smooth and rehearsed similarly.

Rehearsals.
One advantage of chamber theatre is that a performance can be prepared without the lengthy rehearsal times associated with conventional play production where all dialogue lines first have to be memorized together with the learning of multiple entrances and exits before meaningful interpretation can proceed. By using the open text approach rehearsals times can be shorter but the amount of preparation time should never be under-estimated. Fortunately, these rehearsals with a cast of only three or four players will be more intensive than when rehearsing a play with a cast of a dozen or more actors. A single rehearsal with a chamber theatre group can usually achieve more in a shorter time than is often needed at a conventional stage play rehearsal. Mostly rehearsals will take place at the home of the Director or at one of the members of the cast; this is another convenience and cost advantage of chamber theatre.

Chamber theatre players are 'on-stage' continuously throughout a performance and usually have equal amounts of speaking time. These players bond quickly into a team more easily and more quickly than with a conventional stage cast and they are more likely to be equal in their performance skills.

Notes.

1. Berthold Brecht, *On Theatre*, (London, Methuen Drama, 1964), p183.
2. Cicely Berry, *Voice and the actor*, (New York, NY, Wiley, 1973), p22.
3. Steven Guazzo, *The Civile Conversation*, trans. G. Pettie and B. Young, (Constable, 1925) p.138.

8. Performing Poetry.

Poetry can be a natural and powerful element in a chamber theatre performance. A poem may be defined as a piece of creative writing in a rhythmic, and often rhyming, form, usually designed to express deep feelings and thoughts. There is no right or wrong way to read or present poetry. Poetry is feeling, whether written as a ditty, a limerick, lyric, a sonnet or as a narrative poem, and feelings are personal.

Drama is also concerned with feelings and the strict border-line between drama and poetry in terms of feelings and emotion may be somewhat blurred. The words themselves may be understood both in the context of a poem itself and also in the speaker's imagination, understanding and experience. What the poet feels may differ from what individuals in the audience hear. As a presenter/performer of poetry, if you are true to your own understanding and feelings the listener is likely to relate to the words even though the words may be heard from a different experience.

The great wealth of poetry available also provides valuable practice material. Technically, poetry presents a range of challenges and practice opportunities. Making sense of the words provides the foundation for the performance, but the interpretation of the words will involve your use of breath control, timing and pace of delivery in a similar way to performing a prose text.

The first reading of a poem (aloud) will arouse feeling within you; if there is no immediate empathy you may wish to move to another poem at this time. The next step will be to read the poem aloud again with a view to understanding it. At this point you will need to study the punctuation and note especially where the thought or sentence carries across lines; it is necessary to breathe with the sense of the words. This is not something you can learn from a book by rule, but is already inside you as a feeling for words. The fact that you are reading these words indicates that you do have that basic empathy.

Poets attempt to capture emotions in words. Feel the words as you speak, letting the sound of the words flow out and over you. Like a waterfall of sound they may create a picture of beauty in the minds of your listeners and then drop down into a pool of imagination. Understanding and meaning may then follow. In Jill Balcon's words, "Phrasing, lyric impulse, submission of SELF, these have to be drawn out of someone in whom they do exist" (1).

When reading, speaking or performing a poem two elements are always present; firstly there are the feelings expressed by the poet in the words chosen together with the rhythm, rhyme and metre employed, and secondly there are the feelings engendered by the reader performer.

When performing poetry, out of respect to the poet you should look behind the text and try to appreciate the background and intentions of the poet as far as possible. Then you can use the words to express your own reactive feelings.

> "Oh! Leave the Past to bury its own dead.
> The Past is naught to us, the Present all".
> > (*'To one who would make confession'*, Wilfred Scarwen Blunt)

These words are likely to conjure up different thoughts and emotions for each individual, and the way they are spoken can also have different interpretations. Reading and speaking poetry are linked to our own personality and experiences of life.

The structure of poetry.
You will be able to perform poetry more effectively if you understand something about the way verse is structured – the 'poetical grammar'– the style and form of poetry. This does not require deep academic knowledge, only an awareness of the building blocks of verse. Here we can only introduce a few key features. The basic elements of poetry are its metre and rhyme.

The structure and shape of a poem is seen in
- the arrangement in verses,
- the rhyming scheme employed,
- the metrical pattern used.

The elements of a poem include rhythm, accent, duration and pause. Poems are often written with short rhythmic lines (unlike the continuous lines of prose) where the words follow specific accent, or stress, patterns. These lines may be arranged in verses, often based on conventional patterns, or in a variety of 'free' forms which convey the feeling of the poem. The duration of the word sounds and the structured lines combine with the use of pauses to create feeling and meaning. The accent on words may involve a change in pitch of the voice or an increase in volume or tone.

Rhythm is based on the stress patterns of the words; 'the measured undulation of accented and unaccented syllables is the essential feature of verse'. The basic unit of rhythm used in verse is the 'foot' and these are arranged in specific ways; there are five named rhythm patterns.

1. Iambic foot; an unaccented syllable followed by an accented one. English verse in based on the iambic beat, weak – STRONG.

   "I hang my harp upon a tree
     A weeping willow in a lake". ('*Mirage*', Christina Rosetti)

   "John Gilpin was a citizen
     Of credit and renown". ('*John Gilpin*', William Cowper)

2. Trochaic foot; an accented syllable followed by an accented one. The last syllable is often omitted in English verse, STRONG – weak.

   "Now the day is over,
     Night is drawing nigh". ('*Hymn*', Sabine Baring Gould)

3. Dactylic foot; an accented syllable followed by two unaccented ones creating a lilting effect,   STRONG – weak – weak

   "Still to be neat, still to be drest".   ('*Clerimont's Song*', Ben Jonson)

4. Anapaestic foot; a propulsive rhythm creating speed, weak – weak – STRONG.
   The extensive use of dactylic or anapaestic measures tends to become monotonous and variety is introduced by using two-syllable feet, iambic or trochaic.

   "The Assyrian came down like a wolf on the fold
     And his cohorts were gleaming in purple and gold".
                     ('*The Destruction of Sennacherib*', Byron)

5. Spondee foot; two strongly accented syllables, often found in classic poetry, STRONG – STRONG.

Metre and Rhyme.

The metre, or measure, of a verse is determined by the number of feet in the line, and lines are combined into rhyming patterns. Metre is measured in defined stresses, or beats, to words and phrases.

The familiar two-line 'couplet' is rhymed, *aa*.

> "But if the while I think of thee, dear friend,
>   All losses are restored and sorrows end". (*Sonnet 30*, Shakespeare)

> "What is this life if, full of care,
>   We have no time to stand and stare". (*'Leisure'*, W.H. Davies)

Four lines of verse are common and may be rhymed, *abab*, *aabb* or *abba*. Six and eight line stanzas provide almost unlimited rhyming arrangements.

> "Gather ye rose-buds while ye may,
>   Old Time is still a-flying:
> And this same flower that smiles to-day,
>   Tomorrow will be dying".   (*'To the Virgins'*, Robert Herrick)

> "Tiger! Tiger! Burning bright
> In the forests of the night,
> What immortal hand or eye
> Could frame thy fearful symmetry"?
>   (*'Tiger, Tiger, Burning Bright'*, William Blake)

Forms of poetry.

Several forms, or categories, of poems have been described; these include Ballads, Lyrics, Odes, Blank verse and the Sonnet. The poetry of the British Isles is rich in Ballads,

> "There lived a wife at Usher's Well,
>   And a wealthy wife was she;
>   She had three stout and stalwart sons,
>   And sent them o'er the sea".
>   (*'The Wife of Usher's Well'*, Border Ballad)

A lyric poem was originally meant to be sung; now the term is applied to short poems divided into stanzas and which directly express the poet's own thoughts and sentiments.

> "Gather ye rose-buds while ye may,
>   Old Time is still a-flying;
> And this same flower that smiles today,
>   To-morrow will be dying."   *(Robert Herrick)*

The ode is a lyric poem which expresses noble thoughts; it is often written in a lofty style usually in the form of an address or invocation. The metre can be irregular and with or without rhyme.

> "How sleep the brave, who sink to rest
> By all their country's wishes blessed!"   *(William Collins)*

The sonnet.

The Sonnet is a poem built on a basic fourteen lines – usually as iambic pentameter. The rhyming pattern used by Shakespeare is *abab cdcd efef gg*, ending with a couplet.

> "When to the sessions of sweet silent thought
> I summon up remembrance of things past,
> I sigh the lack of many a thing I sought,
> And with old woes new wail my dear time's waste:
> Then can I drown an eye, unused to flow,
> For precious friends hid in death's dateless night,
> And weep afresh love's long since cancell'd woe,
> And moan the expense of many a vanish'd sight:
> Then can I grieve at grievances foregone,
> And heavily from woe to woe tell o'er
> The sad account of fore-bemoaned moan,
> Which I new pay as if not paid before.
>   But if the while I think on thee, dear friend,
>   All losses are restored and sorrows end."
>
> (Sonnet 30, Shakespeare)

Blank verse may be any unrhymed regular measure, but the term is usually applied to unrhymed verse in an iambic pentameter measure. This is the strong, flexible and sonorous verse which Shakespeare explored to great effect, frequently breaking the regularity to meet a specific purpose.

Poetry in performance.

The importance of reading poetry aloud was expressed by the poet W.B.Yeats, "If people are to read poetry at all, if they are to enjoy beautiful rhythm, if they are to get from poetry anything but what it has in common with prose, they must hear it spoken by those who have music in their voices and a learned understanding of its sound".

When preparing a poem for performance the punctuation should be a first guide to its interpretation. Often a sentence will carry on beyond a single line without punctuation so indicating that there should be no pause for breath,

> "Full many a glorious morning have I seen
> Flatter the mountain-top with sovereign eye,"
>
> *(Sonnet 33*, Shakespeare)

Remember also, that there is no strict time measurement in speaking that you find indicated in musical notation; a comma may indicate a short breath but its timing can vary. In this line the speaker can decide the time value of the comma,

> "But, out, alack! . . .
>
> *(Sonnet 33*, Shakespeare)

The individual reader gives a personal time measurement as considered appropriate. At the beginning of Sonnet 54 the reader's own judgement will decide on the value of the comma.

> "O, how much more doth beauty beauteous seem
> By that sweet ornament which truth doth give"!
>
> *(Sonnet 54*, Shakespeare)

Poetry can be very special when presented in a chamber theatre performance; this is a particular event of sharing of feelings with others. For the performer poetry provides opportunities to explore one's own feelings and interpretations – it is also an excellent way to practice breathing and speaking techniques. Whatever the personal feelings of the performer it should always be remembered that each individual listening will have his own personal response to the words and emotions expressed.

Some writers use the term 'speaking poetry' when giving guidance on how poetry may be read aloud. However, poems vary so much in the feelings and emotions expressed that the performer always brings a personal viewpoint to interpretation; in this respect it may be argued that poems are 'performed' rather than 'spoken'. Gross has pointed out that "poetry is not merely the words but what they make happen in the reader's mind" (33) and declares that "the poetry [consists of] mental events evoked by the words, not the words themselves". Cicely Berry regards speaking poetry as being especially valuable to all actors and performers, "it increases [the] sensibility to words, rhythms and meanings which come to you from sound – meanings which cannot necessarily be explained and which go deeper than our conscious logical mind". The poet Basil Bunting was equally explicit, "Poetry, like music, is to be heard . . . it lies dead on the page until some voice brings it to life".

All short poems, and many longer poems, will be fully memorized even though presented as Readers Theatre. It is easier to memorize poetry than it is to memorize prose. This is due partly to the use of rhyme, metre and rhythm and also to the shorter lines employed in poetry, a factor well recognised by ancient Greek performers and the medieval minstrels. But poetry is not just spoken; a poem is an expression of feeling and emotion couched in phrases and sentences that differ in construction and purpose from prose. Sharing a poem with others is an act of performance.

Early story-telling in oral cultures appears to have been delivered in verse form probably using set phrases. In this way long histories could be memorized and re-told. Those early story-tellers were not merely speaking to their audience, they were interpreting the stories as a performance. In contemporary society this ancient practice is continued as 'literature in performance'. The comment made by Clive Barnes after seeing a performance of *Sylvia Plath* about her life and poetry, was that "poetry is what drama is all about. It is the hard core of the dramatic experience – everything else is peripheral documentary" (1); a fact so eloquently demonstrated in the work of Shakespeare.

Notes.
    1.   Clive Barnes, New York Times, January 17, 1974.

9. Players and Audiences.

The intimate performance.
The essential elements of chamber theatre are the small number of players and a small but highly receptive audience. The intimate nature of performing in a small venue requires only three or four players and, when presented in a Host's drawing-room or similar space such as a 'heritage' room, the audience may average around thirty persons. These two factors, so different from a conventional stage play in a public theatre, are significant.

The audience will be selected and invited personally by the Host. This tends to result in a majority of like-minded listeners who will be receptive to this form of performance. The usual economics of conventional theatre become irrelevant; there is no need to select a play or programme with wide audience appeal in order to attract ticket sales required to meet the costs of production. In chamber theatre a small and select audience can enjoy performances of limited general appeal and this may include rarely-seen works including contemporary experimental works.

This is 'literature in performance' and all forms of literature are included, prose, poetry and drama; this inclusive approach takes it beyond the conventional theatre and the performance of plays. Indeed, published play scripts need to be significantly adapted before they can be performed as chamber theatre. However, some plays which may be difficult or expensive to present as commercial theatre can be appropriate and may be arranged and presented effectively as chamber theatre in a small and intimate venue; spoken narration then replaces spectacle, scenery and crowds.

The small cast of players involved enables rehearsals to take place without hiring a large rehearsal room; players meet in their own homes and rehearse in similar circumstances to the eventual performance venue. Rehearsals with three players are intensive with opportunities for a 'practice work-shop' approach, which is not usually practicable with conventional large cast play rehearsals. These few players are likely to bond closely and quickly to create a special sensitive team.

The simple acting area precludes the need for scenery and special lighting. Some performances may use a plain backdrop drape to the players (useful if the domestic wall behind the players would be distracting); this can be simply mounted on a plastic pipe support that is easily transported and erected. More often, no special background is used.

Usually chamber theatre does not require character costumes as in conventional period plays; instead simple black or dark colour clothes may be preferred for the players. Early performances in the twentieth century favoured formal evening wear with the ladies in long skirts and Greek style formality. Sometimes this may still be appropriate especially if the Host and guests are similarly attired; these events can be special occasions, particularly if they are to be for fund raising purposes and the players can reflect this in their dress.

What the players wear should provide a general feeling for the performance or setting, the colour or fabric being appropriate to the 'mood' of the text; dark clothes might indicate tragedy and lighter colour or materials for 'comedy'. This would allow 'indicative' accessories for particular characterisation if needed by the story; these might include the, temporary, use of a veil, fan, feathers, scarf or gloves. If the script requires much action all players may favour black tops and trousers. In scripts where gender needs to be specific the ladies may wear skirts, their length and style being appropriate to both the story and the audience.

In the absence of specific character costumes the players use their acting skills to create character and locality but sometimes a single distinctive accessory may be used; headgear is quick to mount and remove but even a handkerchief or a stick can be effective to accent a character. Masks offer some particularly interesting and exciting possibilities, however, full face masks should be avoided and half-face masks preferred to ensure that speech is not impaired; these may be mounted on a hand-held rod for convenience of use.

Occasionally, simple hand 'props' may be introduced. These must be chosen carefully to be used with a hand-held script. 'Props' are not needed where mime is introduced. Puppetry techniques may sometimes be appropriate. Symbolic devices may represent special objects such as sun, moon or rain. Masks and other hand-held devices become part of the narration. When presenting Chaucer's *Manciple's Tale* the crow in its cage may be stylised to show white on one side and black on the other; this can be turned around at the appropriate time, "*And that's why all crows are black*".

One recommended useful 'prop' is a strong wooden stool; this can be used for many purposes and will provide valuable acting levels to indicate different states and places. It may represent a mountain or a tree, or it can indicate a god or ruler; it may also be used as a simple bench for two players to engage in intimate conversation.

If the available space allows, small portable (folding) boxes or rostra can be useful; these enable the introduction of acting levels and a variety of interpretation devices. The design will be influenced by the requirements of the performing group and the nature of the venues. Heights of six, eight or twelve inches will usually be sufficient as the audience will all be seated around the players. This is 'Theatre of the Imagination' and the presentation and interpretation of a text through words and actions can only be limited by the imaginations of the players involved. The restrictions of the conventional theatre do not apply; images are created in the minds of the audience through words and sound without reliance on physical imagery.

This imagery of the mind requires a close relationship between players and audience where each member of the audience becomes involved with the presentation. Together, these individuals bring their own cultural backgrounds and social issues to a performance and all of these factors can have influence on their interpretation of the performance. The audience is a composite entity and includes both individual responses and a collective response to the performance, "audiences are not passive onlookers, the spectators continue to have minds of their own" (1). The small intimate audience invited by the Host has implications for the nature and impact of the 'audience response'.

To begin.
The character of the performance is established from the moment the players appear and their personal appearance is important. From medieval preaching to contemporary theatre the personality of the 'performer' has always been significant. Chamber theatre does not rely on theatricality but the personality of each player contributes to the way the performance is experienced by the audience.

Players should enter with confidence and good posture, with a smile on the face and in the eyes, all poised and ready, creating anticipation throughout the audience with the expectation of pleasure. They take up position, sitting or standing as arranged. Eye contact will be established between players and audience. Any introduction, speech or narration will provide the opportunity to measure the room for volume and pitch of voice needed.

The advice then is to make yourself comfortable, take a few breaths and relax, calm your nerves and remember this is a friendly group of people and they are here because they *want* to hear your story. It is said that "excitement is more important than theatrics", so flamboyant movements are not appropriate. Convey to the audience that you are excited about your performance and that this particular occasion is especially important – remember that no-one in the audience knows what to expect; you do know what is to happen so get into 'control mode'.

Chamber theatre is always intimate and a shared experience between players and each individual in the audience; it is also entertainment, both the players and the audience should share the enjoyment of the occasion. This relationship is closer than in a conventional theatre. Joseph Grimaldi, the much loved clown, set out to make friends and not mere spectators of his audiences.

Your opening words must gain immediate attention – a single word and accompanying gesture followed by a pause can be effective. The opening words of the text have been selected carefully by the author of the text to gain attention so give these their due value.

Eye contact with the audience is important; each player must be able to see everyone in the audience and must also be seen. Maintaining this contact will help to maintain alertness; this encourages the feeling of intimacy in the performance. The furthest member of the audience will be only a few feet away, feel this distance with your body so that your sheer presence demands attention. Feel alive and be ready from the beginning.

Communicate with the audience before speaking – a head movement, eye contact or gesture will prepare the audience. This will allow you to breathe naturally and 'come into voice'.

To continue.
As you 'tell the story' always be aware of the audience response. Keep in mind that each person in the audience is hearing the words for the first time; your own familiarity with the text needs to be tempered by this awareness. On one occasion a well-known TV personality gave a 'celebrity evening' to an audience of other well-known persons. As the stories were told there were 'cut-aways' by the camera to show audience reactions. The individual responses, laughter at the jokes, also included some individuals who had 'not-sure' expressions on their faces. There may have been issues of inability to hear the words clearly, or insufficient time to assimilate the meaning of the words. Such individual variations of

response are likely to occur in all performances and the factors of culture, age and gender will all influence reactions.

As the story and its performance develops, keep involved with the ideas in the script, act the verbs using appropriate gestures. Communicate the imagery in the text by voice and movement. Be aware of your body language and relate your posture, gestures and movements to the words. Tell the story with your face and hands. Listen to your fellow players and be fully involved in the story and its presentation.

Speak clearly; some exaggeration of the mouth and lip movements can help your pronunciation and so you will be more easily heard and understood by the audience. Keep in mind continually that, although you are familiar with the words and the story, your audience is hearing it for the first time. Use the pause carefully to allow the words to register with the listeners. Don't overdo this as too much theatricality will be tedious.

To conclude.
The conclusion is as important as the beginning. Keep involved with your audience constantly, with eye and gesture, bringing each person into the story – this is an event of sharing and belonging. There will be 'highs' and 'lows' with variations in pace and volume of speaking and you will use all of these to bring the performance to its climax. The words of the script and your delivery will then, in turn, indicate the ending of the story.

A *rallentando*, or slowing down in pace, on the last words or lines, will feel natural; this, together with your body posture and face will allow you to release contact and mark the obvious end of the performance. This is your special 'Amen' as you leave your listeners in a state of enjoyment continuing – rather like a feeling of 'living happily ever after'.

The Audience.
All theatre requires an audience. The act of performance involves the player, the stage and an audience. The 'stage' can be any place where player and audience meet. Acting without an audience is only a rehearsal – or a self-indulgent event with little purpose. The rehearsal is the opportunity to experiment, to explore meaning and interpretation and to develop technique. The presence of an audience is an essential element for a performance and provides the purpose for the event. (In passing, it may be noted that Berthold Brecht early in his career regarded drama as a didactic, a learning tool, and postulated that drama without an audience could be a way in which actors could themselves learn about the world. In

such a case the actors form their own audience and learn vicariously from their characterisation.)

In conventional theatre the audience is an important, and necessary, source of income; the fee for admission is needed to cover the costs of production. To this end a play is usually selected that is likely to have wide appeal to the public, the admission charge is set at an economic level and the performance is publicised and promoted to draw in a sufficiently large audience.

The economics of play production and viewing thus influence the process of conventional theatre. This process can be highly selective and sensitive to contemporary and often local interests. There are limited opportunities in the availability of suitable theatre spaces and only a few plays out of the many thousands written can be performed. It follows that the general public does not have the opportunity to see and experience many great and important works. Even with recordings of plays and films only a small amount of literary works can be seen in a public performance.

The situation may change in future. The Gutenburg Project (1) is creating a digital archive of written literary works and a similar archive of film and theatre is considered but has yet to come to fruition. Two other developments have been initiated which are likely to have significant impact on the access to literature, the Digital Public Library of America (DPLA) and its counterpart in Europe, Europeana. The former project aims to bring about a large-scale public digital library which will unify the continent's major library's resources including the Library of Congress and Internet Archives. Europeana is a similar project aiming to bring together the digital content of European galleries, libraries, museums and archives (2).

Chamber theatre has its own small part to play in bringing some of the world's wealth of literature to contemporary audiences as no recorded archive can replace the direct actor-audience experience.

This growing archive of written material is a valuable source for chamber theatre. With modern technology it is possible to search through a vast range of written texts and then select one suitable for performance. The amount of editing and arranging will vary but working with a digital text can make the preparation of performance scripts easier.

These developments in accessing the original literary texts bring new and exciting opportunities for more people to enjoy the world of literature. It has been well recognised that performing a text breathes life into the words; this can be far more imaginative and compelling than when the text is read silently and alone.

The excitement of performance is created by the simple fact of the presence of the audience. When two or three come together as a like-minded group there is an interchange of attitude and expectation. This is enhanced by the proximity of the participants. If three persons sat widely apart it would be more difficult to create excitement than if they sat closely together; this is the first stage of audience participation. A drawing-room audience is necessarily small in numbers and is seated closely together. This closeness and intimacy of chamber theatre is one of its most potent features and attractions.

Expectation of a special occasion begins with the Host's personal invitation to his guests. Meeting together in the Host's drawing-room and sitting closely with friends and neighbours continues the expectation with a friendly buzz of conversation. This is part of the responsibility of the chamber theatre Host. (This contrasts with a conventional theatre event which can be an impersonal process involving general advertising of the occasion and the impersonal box-office selling of tickets.)

At the appearance of the players the audience falls silent. Without the lowering of house lights as in a commercial theatre, the Host, or the Narrator, begins an opening ceremony with a few words of introduction. This replaces the familiar theatre convention of raising the curtain in a theatre and the discovery of the stage 'set'. A few words only and the action commences as a shared experience.

Because this type of presentation will be novel to many in the audience each person present will be eager to listen carefully in order to follow the story. With the skilled and well-rehearsed encouragement of the players, the telling of the story flows out to everyone present. A chamber theatre audience will have an even closer identity with the story and the players than in a large theatre and their involvement with the players can be intense.

This is 'Theatre of the Mind' and from the beginning of a performance the players bond closely with the audience. The feeling of sharing the story leads to involvement; the players are not observed through a 'glass wall' acting out a play, but in chamber theatre each person present becomes involved and part of the story-telling.

Role of the Host.
The Host of a chamber theatre performance is of critical importance. He, or more usually 'they' as a husband and wife team, will provide the venue – their own drawing-room – and they will invite their guests. This creates the event as a 'private performance' so that the Hosts have control over who attends. Similar comments will apply to performances given in other venues such as libraries, museums, art galleries or 'heritage' buildings; the 'Host' will initiate the selective invitations. The number of guests will depend on the amount and type of seating available. Young guests may be seated on cushions on the floor. Making such arrangements will be familiar to Hosts who elect to host this type of event.

A suitable Host and venue may be found through a charitable organisation who will know of appropriate supporters who have a suitable drawing-room and the interests to be a potential event Host. The seating arrangement should be informal, avoiding any conventional 'theatre style' seating of regular rows. The essence of chamber theatre is informality.

The Hosts are likely to give personal or telephone invitations. An audience of thirty guests may require only a dozen phone calls. This is not onerous to an experienced Host who will almost certainly be used to hosting dinner parties and similar events. If the Hosts wish to raise money for their chosen charity through the occasion, any such donations would be received after the event and would not be part of the performance proceedings.

Refreshments may be provided following the performance and the players may be invited after the fashion of a theatre Green Room gathering. There will be opportunities to discuss the production and its performance and probably some related wider issues. Invitations to perform elsewhere may follow from other potential Hosts.

The Library venue.
Story-telling is a well-established activity in children's libraries; mostly the library staff read the stories but a professional story-teller may sometimes be employed. Children's librarians are dedicated to enthusing young people about literature and this enthusiasm is the foundation of exciting story-telling. Their presentations can be enhanced by an understanding of the elements of performance in the use of the voice, facial expression and gesture as covered in previous chapters.

The professional story-teller will bring a range of creative stories which will extend the resources of the library. The library staff will be primarily concerned to exploit the works available through the library service. This is a large resource which is added to continually by new authors and the only limitation is the time available for such activities..

Every library will benefit from creating its own body of reader/presenters; this should not be difficult as the first resource pool will be the parents themselves. Retired teachers and librarians can be recruited but an even greater number of 'retired parents' is available; any one of these can be the 'lead person' to create a story-reading group activity. In many libraries this is being done already by volunteers; a key group leader can work with the library staff to plan an on-going and developing programme.

Music and song.

Most performances can be enhanced with music which can set the mood or illustrate sections of the story. Bear in mind that the musician and instrument must be 'portable' and you should not rely on a grand piano being available in a performance venue. Medieval works, such as Chaucer's *Canterbury Tales*, may be accompanied by a recorder, or a classical guitar in place of a lute and if a psaltery is not available.

A drum can be used effectively in many folklore tales, such as the Kalahari Bushmen's tale *The Rebirth of the Ostrich*. A native-style 'bongo' drum could be played by a member of the cast. Other sound effects may also be provided by the cast without resort to special sound equipment. Chanting or humming may be used as vocal illustrations to the text.

Although a separate musician may occasionally be needed, songs may be sung by one or more of the players; many actors have good singing voices suitable for a drawing-room. Songs are essential elements in a performance of *John Brown's Body* as the well-known Civil War songs play an important part in the story (these are all available on the Internet). A drum and a recorder (or a tin whistle) can enhance the mood of a performance. Other sound effects can be provided vocally by the players themselves.

A short song can be a valuable connecting link between items in a programme. This may be unaccompanied, perhaps as a duet, or an appropriate musical instrument may be used. Music is always memorable and need not be limited to being 'the food of love'. A mixed programme of poetry and music is a further opportunity to extend the potential of chamber theatre.

Notes.
1. The Gutenburg Project offers more than 40,000 free eBooks online; browse by Author, Title or Language. Founded in 1971, to "encourage the creation and distribution of eBooks". www.gutenburg.org
2. The European digital project website is at www.europeana.eu.

10. Scripts and Arrangements.

Almost any literary text can be arranged for performance and the range of potential scripts for chamber theatre is wide. For effective presentations a few general guidelines may be suggested.

1. Select texts that interest you – they will make better adaptations.
2. Bear in mind your potential audiences – do you wish to entertain specific age or interest groups?
3. Consider the skills and interests of your potential players; a chamber theatre group will be more successful if there is agreement on the general programme and intentions.
4. Books that have already been adapted for film or television may not be readily received by a chamber audience. They are likely to be interested in less-known material.

Poetry.
Poetry provides a rich source of material for performance in chamber theatre. Story poems can be relatively straight-forward to arrange. These are most likely to be written in conventional forms of separate verses, but such divisions can be ignored in the performance script. Very short poems may be memorized and performed by a single player but most narrative poems can be more effective when performed by two or three players. Allocate lines according to the story line and don't be afraid to split a line between speakers.

Read the poem aloud to yourself several times to feel how the rhythm flows. Search for the story in the words used and then read the poem aloud to an audience – a stuffed animal is an ideal audience at this stage; note carefully where a pause can be used.

Very long poems are rarely performed in public; Dylan Thomas's *Under Milk Wood* is popular with many amateur drama groups but Longfellow's *Song of Hiawatha* has been neglected. Presenting great poetry as chamber theatre can be exciting and different; it can be an interesting companion event to the more usual occasions of conventional poetry reading at gatherings of literary groups such as the University of the Third Age.

Apart from Chaucer's works which are of perennial interest, other early stories which would have been recited may have limited appeal. Nevertheless, medieval works such as *Beowulf, Sir Gawain and the Green*

Knight and the *Reynard the Fox* stories will have audiences. Look for translations that are faithful to the poetry of the original text and which read with rhythm. More recent poems offer a wide choice including the works of T.S.Eliot and Robert Frost. Every chamber theatre group will have its own suggestions and preferences from the wealth of contemporary poets and writers.

There are numerous narrative poems for young people, both classical and contemporary which may be equally suitable for older audiences. Robert Browning's *The Pied Piper of Hamelin* is an obvious choice or W.S. Gilbert's *Yarn of the Nancy Bell*. Kipling's *Just-so stories* may also be well received by older folk. All these can be performed very effectively by two players. The range of modern poetry is extremely wide and poems can be found to meet all tastes and ages.

Although narrative poems may come first to mind when sourcing performance texts there is much material which can be collated into a wide range of entertainments. Some suggestions have been outlined below in the section on 'thematic programmes'; such theme topics may include both poetry, prose and song items.

Prose texts.
The vast wealth of fiction available in print, both English and foreign, opens up wide vistas for performance material. Long works will require editing to fit an appropriate time allowance. This may mean omitting some sub-plots or characters and sometimes a principal event.

Because there is so much prose material available in published texts, new contemporary work may be overlooked. In many towns Writers' Groups exist where new writers meet and share their creativity; a chamber theatre group might team up with these writers to perform new works to a wider audience. New writers are constantly exploring human behaviour and developing characters from real-life situations. All this is the stuff of performance; it may involve contemporary life or reflect historical events and personalities. But equally, the writer's imagination may embrace mythological characters or create fantasy and new folklore; the scope of literature is almost unlimited.

Most creative writers write with the 'author's audience' in mind anticipating that their work will be read in the format of a printed book (including eBooks); they are less likely to think in terms of performed literature. A single episode in a story when read silently relies for its interpretation on the experience and understanding of the reader. At a meeting of a Writers' Circle an author might read excerpts of a new work himself indicating a personal interpretation, but a presentation of the work by an experienced chamber theatre group is likely to have a different impact. This might give rise to another name for such events – 'Drama of the written word'.

Collaboration between Writer's Groups and chamber theatre groups could be mutually beneficial. New and exciting material could be presented to wider audiences beyond each separate group. Authors might see their work in a new light and they could see the impact of their words on 'live' readers.

Although some works may be presented effectively by a single gender cast, a useful player group may comprise two male and two female players as this allows flexibility in narration and dialogue. Some stories will indicate one constant narrator but usually the narration can be shared between all the players. The ages of the players may not be critical but in a four-person cast it is often useful to have two 'younger' and two 'older' players; this amount of distinction may help the interpretation.

When arranging a prose script with several characters, it is best not to allocate or designate lines by a character's name as this invites the tendency for the player to identify with the character as in a stage play. General indicators for the speakers might be used such as F1, F2, M1, or simply by letter, A, B, C; this allows flexibility in casting and performance and enables narration to be smoothly merged with the dialogue. In the Performance Texts section below notice how the script for the excerpt from Charles Dickens' *Oliver Twist* is arranged.

Each work should be treated on its own merits and performance requirements. Dialogue may usually be spoken according to gender, men speaking the male parts and ladies speaking the female characters. However, this need not be a fixed rule; in presenting *The Canterbury Tales,* the *Prologue to the Wife of Bath's Tale* can be conveniently shared by two ladies, but in the *Tale* itself a male voice can be introduced and all players will be involved in narration.

Drama texts.
A stage play script might be considered to be easily and readily transportable to chamber theatre use. This is not necessarily so. In conventional theatre the dialogue between actors in a stage play develops the story line and characterisation, but 'scene-setting' in terms of time and place is indicated through the scenery and stage lighting. In a stage play

individual characters are indicated (narrated/described) through costume and make-up. These elements are absent in chamber theatre.

Some of the dialogue in a play-script may describe off-stage events – a device often used in the opening scene – but the actions and movements of the actors provide the principal 'real-time' development of the plot. In chamber theatre these conventional stage devices are replaced by spoken narration. Some playwrights, such as Ibsen and George Bernard Shaw, included 'narration' in their often lengthy stage directions. A play script adapted for chamber theatre performance will often require the insertion of such 'narration'.

A shorter playing time will usually be preferred for a chamber theatre performance and this may require the omission of some minor characters or sub-plots. Very long speeches may be shortened, especially where these are the character's introspections and do not directly develop the story. All such adaptations should start from a careful and detailed study of the text and the intentions of the playwright. The director of the performance will also contribute to the interpretation of the text.

Such text analysis and the creation of a concise performance text should not be so extreme that the result is a 'five-minute show'. Some interesting examples of shortened texts can be seen in Marcia William's cartoon versions of Chaucer and Shakespeare for young audiences although these texts are too concise for performance to adult audiences (see Bibliography). Remember, that when inserting narrative text, a mimed action supplementing the dialogue may represent a complete sentence.

Adapting a published play requires a high degree of editing skill in order to create a text for an interesting and effective chamber theatre performance. The reasons for doing this need to be clearly thought out. One obvious intention might be to introduce a young audience to the works of a classic author such as Shakespeare; in this case the 'adaptation' might follow the pattern of a 'Tales from Shakespeare' approach. Such presentations might also be appropriate for audiences of old people in retirement or care homes. The prose narration would be illustrated with acted excerpts from the play text.

Other instances might be to present complex works that are infrequently seen in the commercial theatre; examples might include *Ondine*, or *The Madwoman of Chaillot* (Giradoux), or *The Chalk Circle*, or *Gallileo*, (Brecht). Such plays as these present challenges as conventional stage productions, but they also present intriguing opportunities for presentation as chamber theatre. Adapting a stage play that is subject to a royalty fee may need specific permission even if it were presented as a private performance.

A drama text is never used in chamber theatre in the full, published play-script form intended for the conventional stage; some adaptation is always needed. An adapted text in its new and specially arranged form may be considered to be a 'new' text. This opens up intriguing opportunities for script writer/arrangers to create the type of texts which can be used in chamber theatre.

Bear in mind always that this is '*Theatre of the Imagination*' and as such there need be no restraints to your imaginative approach to a performance. By now you will be fully aware of the power of words and how they can be interpreted by actors and audience. Music, whether sung or chanted, or a single instrument such as a flute or recorder can add a further dimension to the emotions created by the spoken words.

There is still another dimension which can be considered – the visual imagination.

Typically in chamber theatre the devices of conventional theatre, scenery, lighting and costumes, are not used, but the visual imagination of the audience can be stimulated in other ways. If the players wear 'general style' dark clothes then a distinguishing accessory may be added for characterisation; this might be a chain, necklace or scarf, or using a fan, stick or handkerchief. Half-face masks may be worn to elaborate on a specific character and these might be exaggerations of imaginative design; these are likely to be most effective if worn for only short periods to high-light a particular element in the story. Another visual effect might be to indicate sun, moon or rain (wind can be realistically represented by voice) by devising and introducing an appropriate symbol; this approach may be particularly effective when used in the telling of folk-lore or fairy tales. These devices act as 'triggers' to the visual imagination and should not be complete representations of the imagery.

Compiled (thematic) programmes.
A grouping of items around a specific topic is a particularly appropriate approach for a chamber theatre presentation. This may be described as 'a collage of texts around a theme'. Subjects and methods of presentation are almost unlimited, depending only on the compiler's imagination. This approach has been explored very successfully in the BBC's popular series

of radio programmes *With Great Pleasure*, where several texts, excerpts from literary works, are collated and performed.

Although many texts will arise from the collator's personal knowledge and reading, other sources can be tapped. The Internet and the World Wide Web search engines are valuable tools and can be very productive for ideas and material. Choosing relevant search terms may need a little experimentation and some lateral thinking. Obvious terms will produce well-known material and these may be incorporated as a foundation, but thinking around the topic can uncover material which is fascinating and can lead to unexpected texts.

At first, themes that come to mind might be fairly banal, e.g. 'love and marriage', 'dogs', 'cats', or 'birthdays' (all amusing subjects for a popular performance). It will be more productive to search around on environmental and social issues. History will provide a wealth of material, from particular time periods, specific events and personalities to deeper social trends and aspects of living. Your own interests, knowledge and experience will guide you towards an inspiring collage of material. General abstract 'topics' might include terms such as, acceptance, perseverance, friendship, honesty, compassion, kindness, courage, co-operation and kindness (check these keywords on the Internet for ideas and suggestions). Moral and ethical issues open up wide opportunities as much classical literature is based on such themes. Programmes using this thematic approach can be particularly appropriate for teenagers and young adults and may be combined with a discussion session following the performance. Themes relating to discovery and exploration can lead to almost unlimited ideas for imaginative treatment and available resource materials.

Physical activities offer both serious and humorous treatment, from eating and drinking to running and jumping and all sports and pastimes; explore these in their conventional, unusual or bizarre aspects. The topics of human and animal behaviour open up wide vistas of potential themed material in addition to the more obvious topics of men, women and children in domestic and occupational situations. Cultural practices through the ages will encompass the topics of feasting and celebrations, tattooing and skin piercing to the more bizarre practice of Chinese foot binding.

The work of a single author could be subdivided into topics, chronological or thematic, and then add in multi-author collages. As alternatives to prose authors and poets there will be much material available on musicians, artists and entertainers. The field of science should not be ignored; interesting programmes can be created ranging from cosmology and space to the biology of crabs. Scientific discovery provides unlimited opportunities to explore the science and the persons involved – factual and fun. All these areas will be of particular interest within education where learning can be combined with entertainment and students would research a topic to create a performance script.

Material will be found in books, poems, magazines and newspapers and in a variety of 'reports' produced on a multiplicity of subjects. Judicious and imaginative blending of texts can provide thoughtful and insightful programmes. Successful presentations will always be entertaining, instruction can be laced with humour, poetry mixed with prose, and always music and song can be included for additional, or primary, flavour.

If the items selected are of short duration each one might be presented by a single player alternating with other items. A longer item could involve two players to balance the single items. Keep the overall presentation fluid, using movement as appropriate to avoid a series of static readings. The material itself will indicate the most appropriate presentation technique but the items should be collated carefully into an overall varied and entertaining performance.

Sourcing texts.
The Internet is an obvious and valuable source for texts that may be adapted and arranged for performance as chamber theatre. Complete collections of the works of authors and poets may be read on screen obviating repeated visits to the public library. Much material may be discovered and accessed by searching the network of library online public access catalogues (OPACs). All county public library services will have an online catalogue which is likely to be linked with its book request and borrowing facilities. Many university library catalogues are also available online although direct borrowing of books will be restricted. The British Library online catalogue is the ultimate listing of books in the U.K. as it is the national copyright deposit library and most titles can be available through the local public library network. In the United States of America the Library of Congress serves a similar function.

There are several websites devoted to Readers Theatre itself where much material is available in ready-to-use script form. Such prepared scripts may be useful for school-teachers for use in the classroom but they are less likely to be suitable for adult chamber theatre performances. The texts are often set out in a similar way to a conventional play-script with dialogue lines allocated to specific characters in the story; the number of actors required is thus larger than would be used in a Chamber Theatre performance. This may be useful in a classroom setting as a maximum number of students can be involved in the project.

Researching and arranging scripts is challenging and rewarding. Most Directors will want to do this for themselves, but in a dedicated chamber theatre group one or more enthusiasts may wish to create scripts for others to perform; these could be arranged to suit the talents of their fellow members. In this form of chamber theatre a 'crafted story' approach is followed. This means that the author's original text is used and this is arranged for performance without re-writing.

Script preparation, like any other skill, needs research and practice. The basic story-line will have been provided by the original author and the task is to edit the text into a meaningful format for reading and performance by the players. Although this is fairly straightforward as you follow the story-line through the dialogue and action in the text, you will soon appreciate how the text can be allocated to the speakers. The result may be a performance script similar to a conventional play script but the narration will be spoken by a relevant player, or players, instead of the usual printed stage direction.

Folklore.
When working from an outline story text or synopsis, as often found in the sources of folk-lore tales, the narrative will be edited into the story-line and any dialogue can be added as appropriate. This is the approach used in the script for the Kalahari Bushmen's folk-tale of *The Rebirth of the Ostrich* (see Appendix C). A similar approach will be followed when creating a script based on a non-fiction topic.

Many folk tales can be effectively presented by two players only; gender or age may not be specific although a male and female team can be useful. Using two players has a more powerful effect than a single narrator as the story tends to gain in authority of telling. When creating these scripts, lines may be designated as 'A' and 'B' rather than 'M' and 'F' as this allows the greatest flexibility in casting if a one-sex group is later required.

The temptation to perform folk-tales while sitting should be avoided; this would echo the style of 'bed-time story-telling' and is likely to lack dynamism. Early story-telling would have been accompanied by movement emphasising and illustrating the story action; this is equally relevant to a modern audience. Music is always a useful part of the presentation; this is best kept simple, a small drum and a whistle or recorder can be effective and may require an additional player. The key-note of performing folk tales is sincerity; these early tales were told with authority as part of the cultural beliefs and even today they reflect some enduring truths.

The field of folklore and fairy tales is wide and rewarding. Sometimes only a brief synopsis is available but there are also sources where a tale is fully told. Much of this material can be arranged for performance to young people and also to adult and sophisticated audiences. Indeed, the scope of this field is so great that a chamber theatre group may wish to work almost exclusively in folklore presentations.

Script preparation.
As mentioned earlier, a comfortable size for a hand-held script is A5 size or the slightly larger format 9" x 6" which allows a few more text lines on each page. Ring binders for A5 sheets are available, but these may be cumbersome to handle in performance. The simpler script tablet described earlier is less conspicuous to use than a ring binder as it presents a single page at a time with each turning; A5 page sheets or custom size pages can be inter-changed as required for each performance.

Text lines should be kept relatively short, less than 5" long, leaving clear margins either side. A recommended font style is Times New Roman (TNR) 12 point size minimum. An alternative font style would be Arial 11 point size. TNR is a serif type font which reading research has indicated is easy to read. Arial is a sans-serif font and is widely popular as it has a clean cut face and is familiar to Internet users, it does, however, take up more space on the page than Times New Roman. The players themselves will have opinions and preferences after several performances.

Individual speeches for each player should end at the bottom of the page with the following speaker's lines beginning at the top of the next page; this avoids a distracting page turn in the middle of a speech. The bottom corner of each, or alternate, page may be bent up slightly to facilitate page turning. When using a script tablet a single page is always presented and 'turning the page' is an unobtrusive movement; with a little practice this can be achieved very smoothly.

Stage directions, such as sitting, standing or a specific action, may be hand-written in the margin of the text as would be usual practice in marking a conventional play script at rehearsal. Specific pauses may be indicated by one, two or three slash marks in the relevant place in the text; the number of slashes indicating the relative length of the pause. These marks may be written in with coloured pencil for easy distinction.

Marking a script for a chamber theatre performance may differ from the common practice of making notes in a conventional play script. The latter is always discarded after a few rehearsals as the text and movements are memorized and scribbled notes will be needed for only a short period. The chamber theatre script is 'permanent' in that it will be used at all rehearsals and performances. Script notes should therefore be neatly entered and kept to a minimum so that they are not distracting during a performance. Underlining text is not recommended; if some distinction of speakers is needed simple coloured high-lighting of the player's designation (F1, F2, M1, or A, B, C) is usually sufficient.

Stage directions indicating movements across the 'stage' cannot be 'fixed' as performances will be given in different locations. Players will need to be adaptable to each situation and therefore only general movements will need to be noted. Performances may be repeated over a period of time and inevitably there will be a development of thought with consequent changes in the interpretation of the text; the player's script notes may similarly develop.

It will be appreciated that creating scripts for performance as chamber theatre is both exciting and challenging. The creativity required lies in discovering and recognising the potential of a text and re-formulating it in ways to excite and challenge individuals in the audience. This is not the creativity of Shakespeare but it is rather a new form of creative contemporary theatre presentation.

11. Reading and Communication.

Animals of all kinds communicate through sound or movement; the snarl of aggression or warning, the yelp of pain, the preparatory crouch to an attack and the soft nuzzling of a contented cat are all methods of animal communication. As early man evolved, became upright and fully bi-pedal the way was open, literally, for the evolution of speech. The upright stance allowed the development of the organs of speech, and this was accompanied by developments within the brain to enable the formation of words and language. Communication through speech led to a much wider range of human inter-activity moving through basic information or instruction to a sharing of intentions and ideas and the development of that essential human characteristic of imagination.

Culture and literacy.
Although we cannot know precisely how oral culture developed we can extrapolate from observation of extant primitive cultures that imaginative stories were told both as entertainment and also for edification and the continuity of group identity. These stories continue to provide valuable source material for performance as theatre of the imagination and they can be found in the early folk-lore of tribes and peoples across the world.

The invention of writing enabled the oral elements of culture to be recorded for posterity but this did not replace oral culture. Books had to be copied by hand, a slow, laborious and expensive process. The scarcity of writing materials and low levels of literacy continued into the medieval English scene which was still largely an oral culture. These factors limited the supply and use of written books.

Following the introduction of the printed book to England (1477) there was greater access to literature in its various forms. The earlier, and centuries old, practice of reciting and reading aloud to others began to give way to personal silent reading. The act of reading was no longer a performance, a text interpreted by an entertainer, but it was now the individual reader who brought personal knowledge and experience to discover the author's meaning. The silent reader interpreted the text from within his own personal knowledge and imagination.

The new literacy.
With the advent of the Internet and the World Wide Web there is now a new electronic vehicle of communication and access to information.

Digital technology and the use of smart phones and tablets have enabled new ways to access the written word which can be integrated with visual images and with sound. But this enormous potential has also brought a realisation of its limitations. It is not enough to be able to access vast amounts of information and to download it to create instant books for personal use. A new literacy has emerged – the ability to understand *why* information is needed and how it can be obtained and used. For this process a new term has emerged – information literacy. UNESCO has recognised its global significance and has published a comprehensive 'primer' on the issue (1).

This skill of information literacy is seen as a new competency alongside the basic skills of reading, writing and numeracy. The new competency has been described as 'info-learning', a process of learning about information and how it is needed in order to understand people and life (2). It is a new term for a process that has been fundamental to man's cultural evolution for millennia. The current danger is that with so much focus on the technology we are liable to lose sight of that special hallmark of human nature – our imagination. Reading aloud now has a new importance and potential; the basic principles of 'literature in performance' can be applied to become a foundation for the new competency of 'info-learning'.

Parenting, learning and imagination.
The new literacy, 'info-learning', begins with parenting. Once pregnancy is established the parents-to-be can begin preparation for their new role. In addition to learning the techniques of birthing and baby care, they will begin to explore how they can encourage the development of their child's imagination. The tools for this exploration lie in children's literature and in reading stories aloud – two essential resources on which to build their child's imagination and future knowledge skills.

Through breast-feeding moments, nursing and sleep, parents will sing, recite poetry and tell stories; these are important events contributing to early brain development. Rhythm, rhyme and repetition are basic elements in this development. Story-telling evolves into reading books aloud as the baby progresses to speech and the toddler stage and the process continues throughout the early years. This exploration of learning is accomplished particularly through play. Then the child learns to read and begins to take responsibility for personal reading of books, whilst continuing to be encouraged by both parents.

It is through this world of story-telling that a child extends his world beyond the home circle and encounters other people both good and bad. Through imagination this story world can become very real and influential. As the stories are read aloud with the child, questions are raised to help interpretation of the characters and their actions – '*Why*' is the dominant question – but the other questions quickly tumble out, *Who, What, When, Where* and *How*? As the child grows, these core questions form the basis of future exploration of life and people. This is the basis of 'info-learning'.

Learning through literature.
Moving from parent's reading aloud to the young person's own exploration of books and people brings the opportunities of performing the stories that are being read. Here the child can 'get inside the character' and act out a range of situations outside their normal experience. Learning by vicarious experience through play extends imagination and feelings. Through literature such experiences and emotions are explored by means of words. Prose descriptions clarify and define people and their actions; reading poetry aloud can have a particularly significant effect on young persons by stimulating feelings through rhythm and beyond words.

The words of written literature can be compared with the notes of music. Stories may be told through music, stimulating unspoken feelings and emotions which reach beyond words. The composer suggests this through the musical Key used, tonality of the instruments and directions regarding technique including volume of sound, playing pace and pitch. The musician applies performance indicators to a particular score which are similar to those given to the use of the voice (vocal instrument) in reading stories aloud.

Voice and music.
The human voice is a musical instrument capable of producing a wide range of sounds both pleasant and unpleasant. A musical sound produced on a cello can, with a bow stroke, evoke deep feelings in a sensitive human being. The musical range of the cello is consonant with the human voice and the sounds that it can produce can evoke ecstatic joy or the most intense sadness; Dvořák's *Cello concerto*, B minor (op.104), and Schubert's *Arpeggione Sonata*, A minor, are just two particular examples of music capable of communicating deep emotional feelings. But other instruments can express similar emotions; the breathing of the flute with sweet happiness or melancholy sadness. Even the brassy trombone can be coaxed into a range of expressive sound; each in its own way communicating through the human ear.

The trio of creativity is similar in literature as in music. The ***Author (composer)*** imagines the words, as poetry, prose, (or as musical sounds), which are interpreted by the ***Reader-Performer (musician)*** for the sensitive reception by the ***Audience***. There is both a difference and a similarity between music and speech – musical notes are not as precise as words in communicating ideas but they can be deeply expressive in emotion; both are dependent upon the experience of the listeners.

Reading or speaking a poem requires an audience in order to achieve its full value for its interpretation. A solitary reader derives only a part measure of meaning from hearing his own spoken words. The solitary musician may find meaning by hearing the music being played but the question arises whether the interpreter of music can understand fully the effect of his playing on himself or on others?

To the listener, words have an impact different to music. Words are precise even when they are without meaningful form. In this sentence,

> *"The jangling, rangling of the bells . . ."*

there is a feeling of bells ringing although there is no clear image of their number, shape or size, yet such 'synthetic' use of words may evoke a sense of the discordant sound of a ring of bells being 'rung up' before the ordered ringing of a set of changes begins.

Words communicate meaning by stimulating or triggering a responsive imagery from the listener's memory, experience or imagination. Music conveys feelings which a single hearer can accept and appreciate without the same particularity of feeling as felt by other listeners. Neither the reader or listener can know the exact original image seen by the poet; each creates his own individual response, whether a sound, a visual shape or an emotional event.

> *"Can you hear the whispering of the moonlight"*?

Do you see dark trees gently moving in a slight breeze against a moonlit sky? Is it a country or urban scene? Is it summer or winter, full moon or a new moon?

This isolated sentence needs a context, a preliminary or a follow-up sentence to clarify the intention of the words. But if the words are spoken and are followed by a pause together with a questioning facial expression, a sense of wondering expectation, a feeling rather than an image, can be conveyed to a listener without further words. Sometimes words need to be followed by silence for them to be interpreted by the hearer.

Serious musicians will spend many years learning the technique of playing their chosen instruments. Starting young, perhaps seven or eight years old, there will be hours of practice every day, every week, culminating with a Grade certificate to prove the level of proficiency achieved. But music is not solely a matter of performance technique, it is an expression of feeling. The illustration given by the cellist Rostropovitch in his master-class when he spoke to his student of the empty contents of the very expensive and elegant suitcase is a vivid reminder that it is what is inside the performer that is more important than outward proficiency.

Actors need to practise technique with their own chosen instrument, their voice and body, devoting time and perseverance equivalent to a musician's practice. Greater proficiency will result together with opportunities to explore and find the 'inner voice' which lifts a technical performance to an inspired level.

It is interesting to note how these skills are developed by young people, especially by teenagers. The regular national competition for the Young Musician (BBC) brings outstanding musical talent to light. All twenty-five semi-finalists each time (from an initial list of some five hundred applicants) demonstrate outstanding ability in the mastery of their chosen instrument and their interpretation of music. In contrast, a similar competition for young teenage actors to interpret the speaking of Shakespeare's verse has demonstrated a certain inadequacy in their handling of voice, gesture and interpretation of text.

The young musicians use a 'professional' instrument which, by much practice they play as well as an adult. The young actors use an immature instrument, their own teenage voice, body and imagination, but the difference in comparative levels of performance and feeling with that of the musicians is marked. The young musicians certainly spend a great deal of time in daily practice which is not equalled by the young actors.

These competitions demonstrate that teenagers can have a range and depth of feelings through music equal to (and perhaps beyond some) adults. This appears not to be so in regard to the use of the human voice. Performing Literature enables the exploration of a wide range of feelings expressed in words. Young people need encouragement and opportunity to practise the development of their feelings and emotions through speech.

As the young musician learns the technicalities of the chosen instrument to create sounds and the ability to create music, so the young person needs to learn the use of the voice and the power of words to communicate and to create poetry and prose.

Performing literature as chamber theatre.

Chamber theatre has two noteworthy features; one relates to the audience, and the other to the players. The realm of 'performed literature' embraces poetry and prose and is not confined to conventional play scripts. This provides opportunities for audiences to discover both great classic works and also less known works that may not be performed as conventional theatre. The choice of a conventional stage play for a public performance is always subject to being considered in terms of economics, and where the costs of production need to be weighed against the potential income. The costs of production for chamber theatre are minimal and the small size of the audience enables greater selectivity in the choice of programme.

From the players' point of view chamber theatre creates particular opportunities to develop their performance skills. During rehearsals with a chamber theatre group of three players, the acting experience can be more intensive than occurs with larger casts in conventional stage play rehearsals. The concentrated 'practice workshop' rehearsals enable the players to explore and to become highly skilled in a range of performance techniques.

The number of productions is limited only by the number of Hosts and venues wanting to host a performance. The reasons for hosting an entertainment for a few like-minded friends are many and include providing occasions to raise funds for the many charities and good causes. Potential Hosts might also include libraries, museums or art galleries, heritage and cultural venues and a range of private occasions and events; these may all be linked to the interests of the host organisation. There may be further scope for presentations in the community in parks and public spaces, perhaps in vacant High Street shops. Some of these events may have an 'educational' element within the entertainment; an aspect which may become dominant in a teaching situation.

There is also interesting potential in chamber theatre for 'disadvantaged' players. The wheelchair player can present powerful performances; three chairs on a stage are natural and can create intimate theatre. These players share all the potential of performing with voice, face and gesture with walking actors – there is an advantage of having a built-in lectern. But chamber theatre is also a powerful medium for deaf and for blind players. Performing literary works can provide valuable opportunities for developing voice and communication skills in schools, colleges and universities. The techniques of literature in performance should not be regarded as the prerogative of language departments. Teachers of distinction will appreciate the potential of performance which leads to understanding and no subject need be excluded. Literature and language teachers will recognize the value of performed texts, but themed collages bring other, less obvious subjects, for imaginative presentation. Science and numeracy, both theory and background, can be brought to life through performance. Geography, history and social science may, equally, be presented through the spoken word in a dramatic context. The scope of potential performance programmes is limited only by the imaginations of the teachers and presenters regarding the topics and by the interests of audiences. Whatever descriptive term is used, the essential activity is that of personal and social communication and of understanding people and circumstances. This is a fundamental activity of human life.

Approaching chamber theatre in this way opens up new and different vistas in education and beyond. On the one hand special opportunities are offered to audiences and players beyond conventional theatre. (Amateur drama groups might consider integrating chamber theatre into their regular stage productions programme.) But as a process of 'literature in performance/chamber theatre' it offers exciting insights for education and social inter-action. Speaking words with meaning (interpretation through performance) begins as a simple skill of talking to other people. The personal act of silent reading with imagination evolves into the ability of conversation and social communication (skills well recognised as far back as the Renaissance age). These are skills threatened by the wide-spread contemporary substitution of 'texting' for talking.

The skills of reading aloud, both prose and poetry, can provide a sound foundation for life when introduced early to young children. Through the techniques of performing literature young imaginations can be stimulated and the love of books and reading can be established and fostered. The Education Reform Act, 1988, included the specific clause " . . . children should develop skills not only of reading and writing, but also of speaking and listening".

Denys Thompson feels that our technological society with its 'informational vocabulary', reduces the language that expresses life and our emotions. "The industrial society has created new technological words and hence the way we think. Myths and stories and the symbols of imaginative literature become the "glue which holds together societies and cultures" (3).

In this fast moving electronic age of information it is easy to focus on the technology and its impact on society. But human life is more than technology and technique; it is a sense of 'being'. Throughout the ages men have explored within themselves whilst exploring externally the physical space where they live. In chamber theatre we share thoughts and deliberations in a particularly intimate way across the whole field of human experience.

Performing literature opens up new vistas of life experience taking each viewer/listener beyond their limited personal thoughts and actions. Performed literature is more than reading a book, however vivid is one's imagination. The act of performance takes words and gestures and transforms them into the pleasure of a social occasion – and man is essentially a social being.

Notes.
1. UNESCO, Information for all Programme, *Understanding information literacy; a primer*, (Paris, UNESCO, 2007).
2. Annemaree Lloyd, *Information Literacy Landscapes; information literacy in education, workplace and everyday contexts.* (Oxford, Chandos Publishing, 2010).
3. Denys Thompson, *The Uses of Poetry*, (Cambridge, University Press, 1978) p15.

APPENDIX

A. Sources and Texts.

The most immediate source of texts and materials for chamber theatre performance will be your own bookshelves. Your local public library and the national library network will also be valuable; most County Library Services and many universities have online public access catalogues (OPACS) of their holdings. The Internet can provide access to thousands of texts which may be available online directly or through High Street or online book suppliers.

Some useful websites are mentioned below but this list presents only a fraction of what is available. Use your own selective search terms to find material in specific subjects of your own interests.

Thematic performances are almost unlimited in subject scope. These will be collages of material you collect from your own reading together with additional items sourced from the Internet. Many subjects will be of perennial interest while others may be topical; anniversaries of people and events can be a fruitful source of inspiration and will often come with the idea of a related potential Host – museums, libraries, art galleries, heritage locations or a specific charitable organisation.

Most chamber theatre performances will be classed as 'private performances' in that the audience will attend by invitation and there will be no admission fee. If the Host wishes to raise funds for a good cause then any donations will be handled separately after the event. The significance of this is that royalty fees are generally waived in the case of a private or not-for-profit performance. This allows a very wide range of literary material to be considered for performance and will include both 'classic' and contemporary works. However, although an author may be long dead the copyright and performance rights may be held by a publisher or the author's estate. It is always wise to enquire and to seek permission if there is any question of ownership of the text. (Where an original text is re-worked and arranged for performance this may constitute a new work with the arranger having rights – legal advice may be indicated.)

Novels and short stories provide good sources of material for performance; these will need editing both for time and action. A short story has by definition already been prepared for telling in a short presentation although some will require further shortening. In a 'collage' presentation sometimes only a single page of narrative will be used. This approach was used by Charles Dickens for his public readings from his books; there are plenty of episodes in his novels which provide excellent dramatic performance material. One of Dickens' favourites was the episode in *Oliver Twist* when Bill Sykes kills Nancy. Appropriate episodes can be found throughout literature, both classical and modern.

One potential source of material should be approached with care. Drama texts might be considered to be easy to use, but it should be remembered that drama is story-telling through dialogue and stage action and a play-script has already been arranged for that specific method of performance; some spoken narration will need to be added if a play text is to be used for a chamber theatre presentation. A stage play, typically running for some two hours or more, will need to be edited down and will inevitably lose its distinct theatrical impact.

It may be appropriate for hard-pressed teachers to use a prepared script from the large range of material that has been specially written for Readers Theatre, and this can be a useful introductory approach for use in the classroom. This is less likely to be helpful for an adult group wishing to explore chamber theatre; in this case the initiator may be an experienced Director of stage plays who will have the capability to create a dramatic script. The advice here would be generally to avoid play scripts and select a prose or poetry source for performance. Editing a downloaded copyright-free text will provide valuable experience in preparing a script for chamber theatre.

Most of the suggestions mentioned below for suitable performance material relate to adult works. There is an enormous amount of potential material in children's literature which may be suitable for mixed audiences and is worth exploring. Some children's websites are listed below but there are many more. Always seek advice from the children's librarian in your public library and make friends with local schools librarians; you will find them knowledgeable and helpful.

Literary sources for chamber theatre.
A few well-known literary works are listed below which have been arranged and performed as chamber theatre. These examples are drawn

from older and classic literature but modern and contemporary works will greatly extend the list of potential performance texts.

Chaucer (The Chaucer Experience)
The works of Chaucer, especially *The Canterbury Tales*, are a fruitful source of material for chamber theatre. The *Tales* should be presented in the original manner as an authentic 'Chaucer experience'; three players (1M, 2F) are recommended to provide variety in the performance. There are several modern translations which can be used but Neville Coghill's version (Penguin Books) retains the rhythm of the original verse particularly well. Do not be tempted to use any dramatised play-script version of the *Tales*; this is not recommended as it will not provide a genuine 'Chaucer Experience'.

Two *Tales* may be performed together for an authentic evening of Chaucer; these may be edited for content and performance time to suit the occasion. The following *Tales* have been successfully arranged and performed. In most cases these have been arranged for presentation by 2F, 1M (but alternative arrangements have been made for 1F, 1M, and also for 2F, 2M performances).

> *Canon Yeoman's Tale*
> *Friar's Tale*
> *Manciple's Tale*
> *Merchant's Tale*
> *Nun's Priest's Tale*
> *Pardoner's Tale*
> *Physician's Tale*
> *Reeve's Tale*
> *Shipman's Tale*
> *Wife of Bath's Tale*

Although it is possible to arrange the Tales for performance by only two presenters, adding a third player seems to be particularly effective. A mix of genders for the players is recommended – 2F 1M works well. When performing the *Wife of Bath's Tale*, the *Prologue to the Tale* may be presented by two ladies and then the Tale itself by 2F 1M. As chamber theatre, two ladies sharing the Wife's long *Prologue* works better than a single female voice. This would be different from a conventional stage performance where an actress in period costume might perform the *Prologue* alone and in character. This sharing of a single character by two performers is a useful device in other *Tales*; at the end of the *Manciple's Tale* the 'advice' given as "My mother used to say . . . " is another example. Similarly, in the *Nun's Priest's Tale* the words of Pertelote in the 'dream' sequence can be shared.

If the three players read sitting in the manner Chaucer himself would have used, a lectern may be considered appropriate; this should be of wood although a draped music stand might be used as an alternative. However, shared reading of the *Tales* is enhanced by the introduction of movement and is always to be preferred. Mimed or acted sections can be included – the demonstration of the transubstantiation scene in the *Canon's Yeoman's Tale* is effective when acted out in this way. The cuckolding scene towards the end of the *Merchant's Tale* can be vividly acted by May alone; she might climb onto a wide wooden bench to represent climbing into the pear tree.

Among several translations available, that by Neville Coghill is highly recommended as it is accurate and maintains the rhythm of the original verse. Embedded in the text will be found numerous lines which indicate an accompanying wry smile and glance to the audience – authentic Chaucer? Using Middle English, which a general audience would not understand, would have the effect of turning it into a museum piece; by using modern English the full impact of the contemporary subject matter is felt, e.g. the behaviour of the three young men in *The Pardoner's Tale*, or the greedy deceit of the priest in *The Canon's Yeoman's Tale*.

Benét, Stephen Vincent.
The epic poem, *John Brown's Body* is a powerful narrative of the American Civil War. It was performed as a stage presentation in America in 1954 by three professional actors (2M, 1F) but it is ideally suited to chamber theatre for performance by a cast of 2M, 2F; this latter arrangement is recommended as the story follows the main characters, two men and two women. A separate Chorus of 2-3 persons may be added, or the lines may be spoken and sung by the cast themselves. The evocative songs of the civil war will be an integral part of the performance and can be sourced on several Internet sites.

Longfellow, Henry W.
Though rarely performed, *The Song of Hiawatha* is another rich source of chamber theatre material. Three or four 'songs' may be presented in a single programme and a drum will greatly enhance the presentation. Appropriate action should be included as the repetitive rhythm of the verse may become monotonous. A skilful editor might arrange a conflation of the individual *Songs* for a single performance.

Folk lore and Fairy tales

Folklore, myths, legends and fairy tales are so numerous and such a rich source of material that a chamber theatre group might build a reputation within this field alone. Every nation or culture has its own literature which can be mined for chamber theatre programmes. A search on the Internet will produce online texts and many more published books and collections of stories; see below for some useful websites.

One obvious approach would be to present local or regional folk tales and the public library will be a likely source for material (and a potential performance venue). Taking a multi-cultural view, the choice ranges from ancient people's myths and legends – European, Middle-East or Far East – to more recent creations, e.g. Kipling's '*Just-so stories*'.

Aesop's *Fables* are rich sources for practice in developing texts; mostly these are short pieces but they can be expanded and linked together. The classic *Fairy Tales* of the Brothers Grimm and of Hans Christian Anderson are often suitable for adult presentations as they contain adult themes, but there are many other collections which can be sourced through the Internet and the public library network.

The boundaries between folklore, myths, legends and fairy tales may be a little blurred as you work through them but the classic stories from ancient Greece, Rome and Scandinavia are all important sources. Then, looking further afield to the Middle East, India and the Far East there are many less-known stories waiting to be told. There is a further wealth of folklore from North America, both indigenous and from the early European settlers, and a very wide range of folk stories from the continent of Africa.

Greek literature.

Ancient Greek literature is a rich mine of source material. The so-named 'perfect play' *Oedipus Rex* by Sophocles is a classic work that repays the effort of editing and arranging. For a sophisticated audience, as many chamber theatre audiences are likely to be, such a performance can be a unique experience. Other works by Sophocles, Euripides, and the comedies of Aristophanes also make interesting adaptations, as will Homer's *Iliad* and *Odyssey*. Much of this material is available as online down-loadable texts in modern translations.

Narrative Poems

Two or more narrative poems may be combined with 'mood' poems for an entertaining programme. This short list indicates some of the more obvious possibilities but there are many more to discover, including the works of W.B.Yeats and T.S.Eliot. Modern poets may have copyright or other restrictions on their performance.

> Alfred Noyes; *The Highwayman.*
> Christina Rossetti; *Goblin Market.*
> Edward Lear; *The Jumblies.*
> George Crabbe; *Peter Grimes.*
> John Masefield; *Reynard the Fox.*
> Lewis Carroll; *The Walrus and the Carpenter.*
> Marriott Edgar; *The Lion and Albert* and *Albert Down Under.*
> Robert Browning; *The Pied Piper of Hamelin.*
> Robert Frost; *The Death of the Hired Man.*
> William Cowper; *John Gilpin.*
> William S. Gilbert; *The Yarn of the "Nancy Bell".*

Two useful collections of narrative verse are,
The Oxford Book of Narrative Verse, Opie, Iona, ed. (Oxford University Press, 1983)
The Penguin Book of Ballads, Chosen by Geoffrey Grigson. (Penguin Books, 1975)

Rudyard Kipling

Kipling's '*Just so stories*', although written for children, may be incorporated into an adult programme as they are not really age specific. The stories of *The Butterfly that stamped* and *The Cat who walked alone,* both have relevant adult themes. Other poems which might be included are *The Female of the species* and *The Power of the Dog*. These stories can be effectively presented by two players, 1F, 1M.

German literature.

There are many works of German literature that can make good chamber theatre. The classic *Faustus* by Goethe can be performed effectively and imaginatively in this form and may be preferred to the version by Marlowe. The full text of both versions can be found online.

George Bernard Shaw.

Although the plays of Bernard Shaw might not be generally considered to be appropriate for chamber theatre it may be mentioned that '*Don Juan in Hell*' has been abstracted from the play *Man and Superman* and has been performed separately on numerous occasions and with particularly great acclaim on New York's Broadway, USA.

New Writers.
Local Writers' Groups can be fruitful sources of performance material and a mutually supportive relationship may develop. Make contact and discuss the possibilities.

Libraries and museums.
Every chamber theatre group should endeavour to have a good working relationship with the public library; the members of staff of the children's section likely to be particularly interested. The library will be a valuable source of ideas and textual materials but may also provide event hosting opportunities.

Similarly, museums and art galleries can be potential hosts; performances will be linked to the interests of the organisation. The range of opportunities may cover the materials in the collections or may include special and anniversary events.

B. Performance texts.

The following excerpts from performance texts are intended as an indication of some of the potential of chamber theatre.

An excerpt from *Oliver Twist*, by Charles Dickens

M   [*Introduction.*]

F   There was a candle burning, but the man hastily drew it from the candlestick, and hurled it under the grate. Seeing the faint light of early day without, the girl rose to draw back the curtain.

M   "Let it be," said Sikes, thrusting his hand before her. "There's light enough for wot I've got to do."

F   "Bill," said the girl, in the low voice of alarm, "why do you look like that at me!"

M   The robber sat regarding her, for a few seconds, with dilated nostrils and heaving breast; and then, grasping her by the head and throat, dragged her into the middle of the room, and looking once towards the door, placed his heavy hand upon her mouth.

F   "Bill, Bill!" gasped the girl, wrestling with the strength of mortal fear, "I − I won't scream or cry − not once − hear me − speak to me − tell me what I have done!"

M   "You know, you she devil!" returned the robber, suppressing his breath. "You were watched to-night; every word you said was heard."

F   "Then spare my life for the love of Heaven, as I spared yours," rejoined the girl, clinging to him. "Bill, dear Bill, you cannot have the heart to kill me. Oh! think of all I have given up, only this one night, for you. You shall have time to think, and save yourself this crime; I will not loose my hold, you cannot throw me off. Bill, Bill, for dear God's sake, for your own, for mine, stop before you spill my blood! I have been true to you, upon my guilty soul I have!"

M   The man struggled violently to release his arms; but those of the girl were clasped round his, and tear her as he would, he could not tear them away.

F   "Bill," cried the girl, striving to lay her head upon his breast, "the gentleman and that dear lady, told me to-night of a home in some foreign country where I could end my days in solitude and peace. Let me see them again, and beg them, on my knees, to show the same mercy and goodness to you; and let us both leave this dreadful place, and far apart lead better lives, and forget how we have lived, except in prayers, and never see each other more. It is never too late to repent. They told me so - I feel it now - but we must have time - a little, little time!"

M   The housebreaker freed one arm, and grasped his pistol. The certainty of immediate detection if he fired, flashed across his mind even in the midst of his fury; and he beat it twice with all the force he could summon, upon the upturned face that almost touched his own.

F   She staggered and fell: nearly blinded with the blood that rained down from a deep gash in her forehead; but raising herself, with difficulty, on her knees, drew from her bosom a white handkerchief- Rose Maylie's own- and holding it up, in her folded hands, as high towards Heaven as her feeble strength would allow, breathed one prayer for mercy to her Maker.

M   It was a ghastly figure to look upon. The murderer staggering backward to the wall, and shutting out the sight with his hand, seized a heavy club and struck her down.

* * * *

The Rebirth of the Ostrich.

(A Folk-tale of the Bushmen of the Kalahari desert arranged for chamber theatre.)

Synopsis.

The Kalahari desert. It is a moonlit night. A male ostrich is sitting on his eggs while the females feed. A Bushman approaches stealthily and kills the ostrich taking him home to his wife. She prepares the bird for cooking and discards the short feathers from the breast which have blood on them putting them aside on the bushes.

A breeze comes up and whisks the little feather with blood on it up into the air. The whirlwind blows the feather spiralling up into the air, then drops it into a pool of water. The feather curls up and stretches out. It becomes a small ostrich and begins to grow. As his legs form, the little male ostrich steps out of the water and looks for food. He finds leaves on the bushes close to the ground. As he grows larger he can reach up and feed from the higher branches. His bones begin to harden and he grows stronger. Now he is a fully grown male ostrich. He searches for a mate. He calls out and the females join him. They scratch out a home in the ground and lay their eggs.

The male ostrich sits on the eggs while the females forage for food. A jackal approaches to seize the eggs. The ostrich kicks out and with a howl the jackal slinks away. The ostrich sits and waits. New life has come to the desert.

Performance script (excerpt).

The Rebirth of the Ostrich

(A Folk-tale of the Bushmen of the Kalahari desert arranged for chamber theatre.)

Introductory music – drums and wind instruments of Africa.

M   A hot wind is blowing across the desert.

F   This is the Kalahari desert of South-West Africa;
         Dry and dusty.

M   It is night.
         Black night with the diamond stars above.

F   The rocks of the desert are still warm from the sun.
         The few scrub trees huddle above the rocks,
         Their sharp thorns pierce the hot wind.

M   The desert deserted.
         Only the sound of the restless wind,

F   and the distant roar of a lion.

M   The deathly desolation of the desert.

F   But there is life.
Beneath a scraggly thorn tree sharp against the moon,
                             there is an ostrich.

M   It is a male ostrich.
He is sitting on his eggs.

F   A faithful father, he is the protector of new life to come.
His consort is away.
She has sat all day and now takes her turn to feed.

M   He is alone.

F   But he is not alone.
He is in danger –

M   there is a hunter abroad.
This is the most aggressive of all hunters –

F   it is man!

M   This is the law of the desert.
Each living creature must eat.

F   And this man is hungry . . .

* * * *

John Gilpin
William Cowper

M   John Gilpin was a citizen
         Of credit
F   and renown,
M   A train-band captain eke was he
         Of famous London Town.

F   John Gilpin's spouse said to her dear,

         'Though wedded we have been
         These twice ten tedious years, yet we
         No holiday have seen.

         'Tomorrow is our wedding-day
         And we will then repair
         Unto the Bell at Edmonton,
         All in a chaise and pair.

         'My sister and my sister's child
         Myself, and children three,
         Will fill the chaise; so you must ride
         On horseback after we'.

M   He soon replied,

                 'I do admire
         Of womankind but one,
         And you are she, my dearest dear,
         Therefore it shall be done.

         'I am a linen-draper bold,
         As all the world doth know,
         And my good friend, the Calendar,
         Will lend his horse to go'.

F   Quoth Mrs. Gilpin,
                 'That's well said;
         And, for that wine is dear,
         We will be furnished with our own,
         Which is both bright and clear'.

M   John Gilpin kissed his loving wife;
          O'erjoy'd was he to find
          That, though on pleasure she was bent,
F   She had a frugal mind.

M   The morning came, the chaise was brought,

F   But yet was not allowed
          To drive up to the door, lest all
          Should say that she was proud.

M   So three doors off the chaise was stay'd,
          Where they did all get in . . .

*****

The Pied Piper of Hamelin

Robert Browning

This is a story about a magical piper and a plague of rats!

M1   Hamelin Town's in Brunswick,
        By famous Hanover city;

F1   The river Weser, deep and wide,
        Washes its wall on the southern side;

F2   A pleasanter spot you never spied;
        But, when begins our ditty,
        Almost six hundred years ago,
        To see the townsfolk suffer so
        From vermin, was a pity.

M1   Rats!
        They fought the dogs and killed the cats,

F1   And bit the babies in the cradle,

M1   And ate the cheeses out of the vats,

F2   And licked the soup from the cook's own ladles,

F1   Split open the kegs of salted sprats,

F2   Made nests inside men's Sunday hats,

M1   And even spoiled the women's chats
        By drowning their speaking
        With shrieking and squeaking
        In fifty different sharps and flats.

F2   At last the people in a body
        To the Town Hall came flocking:
        "'Tis clear', cried they , 'our Mayor's a noddy;
        And as for our Corporation –

F1   shocking
        To think we buy gowns lined with ermine
        For dolts that can't or won't determine
        What's best to rid us of our vermin!
        You hope, because you're old and obese,
        To find in the furry civic robe ease?

F2   Rouse up, sirs! Give your brains a racking
To find the remedy we're lacking,
Or, sure as fate, we'll send you packing'!

F1   At this the Mayor and Corporation
Quaked with a mighty consternation.

M1   An hour they sat in council,
At length the Mayor broke silence;
'For a guilder I'd my ermine gown sell,
I wish I were a mile from hence!

It's easy to bid one rack one's brain –
I'm sure my poor head aches again,
I've scratched it so, and all in vain.
Oh for a trap, a trap, a trap'!

F2   Just as he said this, what should hap
At the chamber door but a gentle tap?

M1   'Bless us', cried the Mayor, 'what's that'?

F1   (With the Corporation as he sat,
Looking little though wondrous fat;
Nor brighter was his eye, nor moister
Than a too-long-opened oyster,

F2   Save when at noon his paunch grew mutinous
For a plate of turtle, green and glutinous.)

F1   'Only a scraping of shoes on the mat?
Anything like the sound of a rat
Makes my heart go pit-a-pat'!

M1   'Come in'! the Mayor cried, looking bigger:

F2   And in did come the strangest figure!
His queer long coat from heel to head
Was half of yellow and half of red . . .

*****

128

C. Internet source websites.

Book texts available online.
//Online books.library.upenn.edu
More than 10,000 book texts, free access.
Author – title – subject – serials indexes.

//Archive.org.details/texts
Online book texts listed as U.S.A., Canada, and Universal libraries.
Author and Title indexes.

www.bibliomania.com
More than 2,000 classic book texts, including short stories.

www.classicreader.com
Free online books, including Fiction, Short stories, Poetry and Young readers.

www.forgottenbooks.org
Categories listings.
50 free downloads, thereafter a membership fee is required ($0.02 per book)

www.fullbooks.com
Online book texts; includes German language books. Titles index.

www.gutenburg.org
More than 40,000 book texts, free access; e-books including Kindle books. Category listings. Includes short stories.

www.ipl.org/reading/books
Internet Public Library.
Subject search. Search engine to other book text websites.

www.justfreebooks.info
A search tool to more than 700 websites to access free online books.

www.shakespeare-online.com
Complete works of Shakespeare, texts and notes.

www.opensourceshakespeare.org
Information source about Shakespeare and his works.

www.luminarium.org
Excellent source of information about Chaucer and *The Canterbury Tales*, including full text.

www.librarius.com
Comprehensive site on Chaucer with links to other relevant information.

Online Poetry websites.
www.daypoems.net
An archive of public domain poetry texts, includes the works of Blake, Rupert Brooke and Oscar Wilde.

www.dmoz.org/arts/literature/poetry
The Bibliomania Poetry Archive; poems in the public domain. Lists 31 searchable collections of poetry, including Bibliomania Poetry Archive and Bartleby collections.

www.bartleby.com
A major collection of poetry, American and English 1250-1920.

www.coffeehousepoetry.org
A London based organization.

www.poemhunter.com
A search engine to sources of poetry texts.

Online Folklore websites.
(Folktales, Fables, Myths and Legends)

// myths.e2bn.org
Myths and legends of the British Isles.

www.americanfolklore.net
Title index with categories listing.

www.aaronshep.com
A very large collection of texts with categories index including Readers Theatre scripts; material suitable for children and classroom use.

www.pitt.edu
A source for folklore and mythology titles including electronic texts. Excellent site with links to some of the most useful search engines.

//myths.e2bn.org
Sources for myths and legends of the British Isles.

//teacher.scholastic.com
Advice on writing one's own folk-tales.

Short stories.
www.bergtraum.K12.ny.us

Children's literature.

www.childrensbook.me.uk
Reading to babies and young children, benefits and reading lists – Babies
- 5years old, Boys and Girls.

www.earlyreadingskills.co.uk
Advice on developing reading skills for ages 1-10years.

www.goodsitesforkids.org
Useful information source for parents and teachers.

www.mvcc.libguides.com
Reading guides to children's books.

www.rnib.org.uk/living with sight loss
Help and courses available on Braille for children and young people.

Tongue twisters.

www.buzzle.com
Tongue twisters for adults.

www.fun-with-words.com/tongue_twisters
This collection includes long tongue twisters.

www.tongue-twisters.org
A collection of more than 2,000 tongue twisters.

//thinks.com/words/tonguetwisters
Well-known tongue twisters including funny ones.

//sembj.hubpages.com/hub/A-Tongue-Twister-is-more-than-just-a-joke
Advice on learning and saying tongue twisters.

Reading and speech websites.
www.readingonline.org
Free online publication of the International Reading Association (IRA) a professional organisation of literacy educators. The focus is on practice and research in the classroom (ages 5-18).

Story-telling websites.
www.sfs.org.uk
The Society for Story-telling (England and Wales).

www.storynet.org
U.S.A. National Storytelling Network (NSN).

www.scottishstorytellingcentre.co.uk
Story-telling in Scotland.

www.australianstorytelling.org.au
The Storytelling Guild of Australia.

//storytelling.org.nz
The New Zealand Guild of Storytelling.

www.sc-cc.com
Storytellers of Canada / Conteurs du Canade (bi-lingual site)

www.verbalartscentre.co.uk
Derry, Northern Ireland (Hosts of Storytellers of Ireland).

www.pjtss.net/ring
The Storytelling Ring, lists all members (177 sites).

www.pitt.edu/~dash/grimm
Primarily dedicated to the works of the Brothers Grimm.

www.timsheppard.co.uk
Wide range of storytelling material listed (varying quality).

Readers Theatre.
www.aaronshep.com
Useful resource about Readers Theatre.

www.teachingheart.net
Readers Theatre scripts and plays.

www.scriptsforschools.com
Lois Walker's online shop for a wide range of prepared scripts for
Readers Theatre.

Bibliography.

Bauer, Susan Wise, *The Well trained mind*. (New York NY, Norton, 3ed. 2009).

Bennett, Andrew, *An Introduction to Literature Criticism and Theory*, (London, Longman, 4ed. 2009).

Berry, Cicely, *Voice and the actor*. (New York, NY, Wiley Publishing, Inc.1973).

Bleek, W.H.I. and L.C. Lloyd, Specimens of Bushman Folklore. (London, George Allen & Company. [1911]. Resurrected by Abela Publishing, London, 2009).

Breen, Robert S, *Chamber Theater*, (Englewood Cliffs, NJ., Prentice-Hall.1978).

Briggs, K., *A Dictionary of British Folk Tales in the English Language*. (London, Routledge and Kegan Paul. 1970).

Esslin, Martin, *The Field of Drama*, (London, Methuen Publishing Ltd., 1987).

Frye, N., *Anatomy of Criticism.* (Princeton, NJ; Princeton University Press, 1957).

Furniss, T.E. and Bath, M., *Reading Poetry; An Introduction*. (London, Longman, 2ed. 2006).

Guerber, H.A., *Middle Ages*. (London, Studio editions, 1994).

Houseman, Barbara, *Finding your voice*. (London, Nick Hern Books, 2002).

Joseph, Stephen, *Theatre in the Round*. (London, Barrie and Rockliffe, 1967).

Krauss, Kenneth, *Private Readings/public texts; playreaders' constructs of theatre audiences.* (London, Associated University Presses, 1983).

Linklater, Kristin, *Freeing Shakespeare's Voice: the Actor's Guide to Talking the Text*. [1992].

Lloyd, A., *Information Literacy Landscapes; information literacy in education, workplace and everyday contexts.* (Oxford, Chandos Publishing, 2010).

Lloyd, L.C., ed. *Specimens of Bushman Folklore*. (London, George Allen & Co., 1911, Resurrected by Abela Publishing, London, 2009).

Markowitz, Arthur, *With Uplifted Tongue.* [n.d.]
(Poems, songs and fables of the Bushmen of South Africa).

Montgomery, Martin, Alan Durant, Nigel Fabb, Tom Furniss and Sara Mills, *Ways of reading; advanced reading skills for students of English literature*. (London, Routledge, 3ed. 2007).

Ranger, Paul, *Meaning, Form and performance; a guide for Bronze, Silver and Gold medal candidates (The speaking of verse and prose) and ALAM Recital Diploma Candidates*. (London, Oberon Books Ltd. 1995).

Ratliff, Gerald Lee, *Introduction to Readers Theatre; a guide to classroom performance*. (Colorado Springs, CO. Meriwether Publishing Ltd. 1999).

Rodenburg, Patsy, *The Actor Speaks; voice and the performer*. (London, Methuen Drama, 1997).

Thompson, David W, *Performance of literature in historical perspective*. (Lanham, MD, University Press of America Inc, 1983).

Trinity Guildhall, *Acting and Speaking, Graded Examinations, Performance Certificates, Syllabus from 2010*. (London, Trinity Guildhall, 2ed. 2010).

UNESCO, Information for All Programme, *Understanding Information Literacy; a primer*. (Paris, UNESCO, 2007).

Vitz, Evelyn Birge, *Teaching Arthur through performance.* see the website, www.nyu.edu/projects/mednar/vitz (This prolific scholar and teacher has written extensively on the topic 'Literature in performance').

Williams, Marcia, *Tales from Shakespeare*, London, Candlewick Press, 1998).

Index

www.ingramcontent.com/pod-product-compliance
Lightning Source LLC
Chambersburg PA
CBHW072134280526
45788CB00002B/637